Twayne's United States Authors Series

Sylvia E. Bowman, *Editor*

INDIANA UNIVERSITY

Anne Bradstreet

ANNE BRADSTREET

by JOSEPHINE K. PIERCY

Indiana University

 72

Twayne Publishers, Inc. :: New York

MANUFACTURED IN THE UNITED STATES OF AMERICA BY
UNITED PRINTING SERVICES, INC.
NEW HAVEN, CONN.

To My Students
who have "discovered"
Anne Bradstreet and her
contemporaries.

Preface

ANNE BRADSTREET, the "tenth muse" who sprang up in America at a most unlikely time, is the subject of this study. The years between 1630, when she came to America with the Massachusetts Bay Company, and 1650, when her volume of poetry was published, were most unpropitious for creative effort of any kind in New England. The towns of Newtown, Agawam, and Merrimac, the places of her residences, were, like other colonial towns, nestled in a wilderness. America was not ripe for the creation of poetry or any other of the arts, not so much that the Puritans were against them as that the essential business of living left neither time nor a sympathetic environment for such endeavors. And for a woman to write poetry was unheard of.

Yet the fragile woman of this study—the daughter of Governor Dudley, the wife of Simon Bradstreet who became a governor, and the mother of eight children—stole time from her official and domestic duties to write a considerable volume of poetry, and by so doing became not only the first British American to publish a volume of verse but the first English woman to have a volume of durable poetry published. In spite of weaknesses in her verse, it has endured, going through several editions into the nineteenth century and through reprints even into our own time.

It seems strange, therefore, that there has not been an adequate biography of the poet or a separate critical study of her work. There have been excellent appreciative paragraphs introducing selections from her work in anthologies, a sympathetic analysis by Moses Coit Tyler in his *History of American Literature*, and an admirable introduction by John

Harvard Ellis in his scholarly edition of the poems in 1867, but that is as far as criticism has gone.

Such comparative neglect leaves a fresh field for analyses of a book that is important not only as a historical phenomenon but also as a real contribution to American literature. It is important, too, as a study of a Puritan woman who could not always accept the doctrines of her contemporaries.

The present analysis, therefore, takes on two aspects. The first is an analysis of the Bradstreet poetry and prose for their revelation of the author's spiritual growth in her own very personal struggle with orthodoxy. This is discussed in the chapter "The Christian Pilgrimage." The second is the study of Anne Brastreet's development as a writer from her imitative apprenticeship to her maturation as a true poet who anticipated the English Romantic poets and who may very well have been read by them.

I am indebted to many people for kindness and assistance in creating this study and to publishing firms for their permissions to quote from various books. I wish to thank Mr. William Jackson, Mr. William Bond, Miss Caroline Jakeman for their information at the Houghton Library at Cambridge; Miss Barbara Simison of the Sterling Memorial Library at Yale; and particularly the staff of the Lilly Library at Indiana University—Mr. David Randall, Miss Geneva Warner, Miss Doris Reed, Mrs. Constance Work, Miss Elfreda Lang, Mrs. Dorothy Shive, and Mrs. Vonnie Nicholls—who have had to put up with me for the greater part of a sabbatical year. Most of all, I wish to thank Mr. Buchanan Charles for the privilege he gave me of examining the only extant manuscript in the handwriting of Anne Bradstreet. His enthusiasm for Mistress Bradstreet is contagious. Also, Miss Marion Batchelder of the Stevens Memorial Library at North Andover, showed me other Bradstreet items.

I am greatly indebted to Professor C. L. Barber and Professor Edwin H. Cady of Indiana University for their encouragement in undertaking this project and especially to Professor

Emeritus Frank Davidson, whose suggestions and criticisms were invaluable. He encouraged me in my belief that Anne Bradstreet had read Shakespeare, adding to my own illustrations, for instance, the similarity of a Bradstreet stanza to a Shakespeare sonnet and other similarities to the line on the asp in *Antony and Cleopatra* and another passage in *The Winter's Tale*. He reminded me, also, of medieval debate literature.

I wish to acknowledge the following persons and publishers for their kind permissions to quote from some of their texts: Appleton-Century-Crofts, *Century Readings in American Literature,* edited by Fred Lewis Pattee; Barnes and Nobles' edition of Winthrop's *Journal,* edited by James Kendall Hosmer; Blaisdell Publishers and Ginn and Company, Percy Boynton's *Literature and American Life;* the Collectors' Bookshop (Seven Gables Bookshop) and Mrs. Whicher from George Frisbie Whicher's *Alas, All's Vanity;* Farrar, Straus & Company, Inc., John Berryman's *Homage to Mistress Bradstreet;* Houghton Mifflin, Samuel Eliot Morison's *Builders of the Bay Colony;* the Johns Hopkins Press and Mr. Wright, Louis B. Wright's "The Purposeful Reading of Our Colonial Ancestors," which appeared in *E L H;* New York University Press, Samuel Eliot Morison's *The Puritan Pronaos;* and the *William and Mary Quarterly* and Miss Elizabeth Wade White, her article on Anne Bradstreet.

Contents

Chronology

1612 Birth of Anne Dudley, daughter of Thomas Dudley
      and Dorothy Yorke Dudley, supposedly at Northampton, England.

1619- Thomas Dudley and family in household of Earl of
1630   Lincoln where Dudley was the earl's trusted steward
       and friend. Interval in 1628-29, Dudley in Boston,
       England.

1628 Anne married to Simon Bradstreet, also under patronage of the Earl of Lincoln.

1630 Bradstreets and Dudleys sail in *Arbella* with other
      Puritans to settle in Massachusetts Bay. Quick moves of
      residence in New World from Salem to Boston to
      Cambridge.

1631 Spring, settle in Newtown (Cambridge).

1635 Move to Agawam (Ipswich).

1638- Some time in this period move to Merrimac (Andover),
1644   which becomes permanent home.

1647 Reverend John Woodbridge sails for England, possibly
      carrying manuscript of Bradstreet poems with him.

1650 *The Tenth Muse Lately Sprung Up in America* published (London).

1672 September 16. Death of Anne Bradstreet.

Anne Bradstreet

CHAPTER *1*

Prologue

IN 1650 THERE APPEARED in London an unpretentious-looking volume of poetry with a very pretentious title, *The Tenth Muse Lately Sprung Up in America*. The author, Anne Bradstreet, was surprised and embarrassed at her elevation among the muses, for the book had been published without her knowledge through the efforts of an admiring brother-in-law who had carried the manuscript off to England. His judgment was not altogether bad, although the poet herself saw the necessity for revisions and additions that led to the second (the first American) edition in 1678, six years after her death.

Anne was a Puritan woman of deep spiritual faith, but her highly intelligent and well-educated mind was capable of questioning and even of rebellion. Her unusual background made her that way.

The facts we know about her are few, but they have significant bearing upon her work. She was born in 1612 supposedly in Northampton, England.[1] Nothing is known about her mother's life or character except as Anne suggests it in her epitaph for her. The record of her father, Thomas Dudley,[2] was destined, however, to go down in the pages of American colonial history. Left an orphan at ten, he served as a page in a distinguished household and as a soldier under Queen Elizabeth in her alliance with France against Spain. In his religion, he became a nonconformist; in his career, a capable administrator. In 1619, the Earl of Lincoln chose him as his steward to manage his affairs. Except for a short interval, Dudley held that position until 1630, when he sailed with his family for America with the Massachusetts Bay Company.

Also in the Earl of Lincoln's household was another of his protégés, Simon Bradstreet, who, left an orphan when he was fourteen, came into the Earl's service a few years later and was put under the supervision of Dudley. The careers of Dudley and Bradstreet were parallel in kind if not in time. Both became stewards to the Earl of Lincoln, both came to America in 1630, both served as capable administrators and governors of the Massachusetts Bay Colony.

The castle of Sempringham, the Earl's residence, would seem an ideal background for romance, and so it must have been. All we know is that Anne Dudley and Simon Bradstreet were married in 1628, when she was sixteen and he twenty-five. Again history, as written by others, records nothing of their life together; but we know from her poems, the best source of all, that theirs was a supremely happy marriage.

Together with the Dudleys they undertook the great adventure to America. The voyage, though lacking the complete uncertainties and foreboding of the first settlers' journey, was not easy, particularly for those, like Anne, who had led gentle lives in England. They set sail from England on March 20, 1630, and did not reach their destination until three months later. The *Arbella*, on which the leaders of the company sailed, was a three-hundred-fifty-ton vessel. Winthrop's *Journal*[3] records their anxiety at sea over stormy gales and becalmed seas and the constant danger of enemy ships. Some passengers were sick; a few died at sea. Others, like Lady Arbella, for whom their ship was named, found the experience too rough and died on land within a year.

Some friendly English people, however, were on hand to greet the newcomers and to help them get settled. The towns of Salem, Boston, Newtown (Cambridge), and Agawam (Ipswich) were already established and were to become, in succession, the places of residence of the Dudleys and the Bradstreets. Although civilization, of a frontier sort, awaited them and they were therefore more fortunate than the first comers, life was difficult. Sickness and death were ever present. The winters were freezing cold. The land was rocky and almost untillable, and crops, subject to the land and the weather, were uncertain. Beyond the villages was the inevitable forest inhabited by Indians. Some were friendly and helped the English settlers in time of trouble, but for every one of these there were others on the warpath against the white people who had usurped their land. It was no wonder that Anne Bradstreet's heart rose at this new world and its new manners. There was no castle with its well-furnished and pleasant rooms nor a Lincoln estate with its beautiful English gardens.

The colonists had to work and pray to establish a kingdom of God in a wilderness, the purpose for which they came to America. They were a determined people. They had come to found a new Canaan, where they might worship according to their own doctrines. America was the promised land. In England they had turned from the trappings and ceremony of the Anglican Church because these reminded them too much of the Catholic Church, which the Protestants had rejected. They wished to return to simple, plain religion, unhampered by symbols, as they felt Christ had intended. Their ministers, being men of conviction, practiced what they preached; and for failure to wear the surplice or to follow some other ceremony they were mentally and physically persecuted and sometimes sent into exile. Archbishop Laud and his agents, ever zealous to seek out and punish dissenters, sometimes cut out the tongues of offenders so that they could preach no more. Those who would worship in the unadorned way had to seek a new home.

In a sense, there was no more appropriate setting for plain religion than a new colony unhampered by custom or tradition. It suited and enhanced it, for there was neither time nor opportunity to build cathedrals even if, by the remotest chance, they might have felt some nostalgia for those towering edifices of England. The simple meeting house did for both church and state until better days. Even so their simplicity had a certain beauty that has influenced church architecture in America ever since.

The harsh environment re-emphasized, too, some of the most severe aspects of their doctrines. Satan, jealous of their gift of a new Canaan, was abroad in the land, sometimes in the guise of an Indian, sometimes as a witch, sometimes in the waywardness of an individual. But there was present, too, the Just Judge, who could intervene personally in the affairs of man, meting out punishment when it was due or rewarding the faithful. He could be prayed to as an Immediate Presence, and He could answer the prayers as He seemed very often to do. If the personal plea was not granted, the supplicant did not doubt, for to the Puritans the ways of God, though sometimes inscrutable, were always just. They believed in an all-wise God, who ruled the universe. Without the cynicism of the eighteenth century's mechanistic concept that "whatever is, is right," they accepted His decrees whether they boded good or ill.

In their harsh environment, it might be expected that Calvinism would flourish, but in its severest form it did not, except among a few like the Reverend Michael Wigglesworth who vividly portrayed its most forboding aspects in his *Day of Doom*. It seems a blessing that Anne Bradstreet did not live long enough to read that terrifying poem. In its most orthodox form, Calvinism taught that there had been a covenant in the Garden of Eden between God and his new creatures. They could live in eternal bliss if they obeyed God. But they broke the covenant by eating of the Tree of Knowledge and were driven out of the Garden with a curse upon them and all their descendants, who would be born forever utterly depraved. However, theorized the Calvinists, the all-wise and merciful God ultimately elected to save a few by sacrificing his only Son so that they might receive grace. Who they were was predetermined and unalterable. Not good works but grace alone could save them. This was the orthodoxy condemned by William Ellery Channing in the early nineteenth century. It was the orthodoxy of those Puritans who conceived their Deity as an avenging, sometimes angry and terrifying God.

Most New England Puritans, however, accepted limited Calvinism. Their personal God was not so terrifying as strict orthodoxy would make Him. Although man in Adam had merited God's everlasting anger, His love was infinite. There was always the hope that one might be among the chosen. Such a one, however, could not benefit from grace until he became united with Christ through the Holy Spirit's effect upon him. To achieve this he would walk in the path of righteousness, he would learn the ways of God through preacher and teacher, he would understand and be uplifted by participation in Holy Communion. It is the theme of conversion then, and the "marriage" of the soul to Christ that becomes the subject of many Puritan sermons and meditations, the most popular media for the propagation of the Gospel. In fact, Christian doctrine and the ways of God to man, as might be expected, are the all-consuming topics of every form of reading and writing among the Puritans of New England: the journal, as current Christian history in America; the diary, as a daily record of God's activity in the affairs of man; history, for moral lessons to be derived from man's evil and his goodness; poetry for prayer and testimony of God's omnipotence. Whether one wrote or read, one remained ever aware of the eye of God.

However narrow and too consuming such attitudes seem to us now, the mental and moral discipline was excellent. Ever alert to new manifestations of God, the Puritans became our first scientists as they scanned the heavens and found that they did, indeed, declare the glory of God. Their minds were receptive to the theories of Galileo, Copernicus, and

Kepler. As far as their knowledge could lead them, their eyes and their minds took in the universe as well as their own planet. And on their own planet, they saw God all about them. This awareness of God in nature permeates the later poetry of Anne Bradstreet.

The New England Puritans, in spite of their orthodox views, were people of broad intellect. They were, after all, the products of Elizabethan and seventeenth-century England. It is doubtful that they forgot or lost the influence of their background. Only the harsh circumstances of their persecution and their difficult living made them hide their happier breeding under the somber cloak of Puritanism.

England in the early seventeenth century was a fortunate place and time for our future American poet to have spent the first eighteen years of her life. The Puritans who were to sail to America in 1630, with the Dudleys and Bradstreets among their number, were by birth and culture Elizabethans. These American immigrants stepped from the most glorious period of English history and literature. Horizons were expanding far beyond the British Isles, and the exploits and explorations of men like Sir Francis Drake and Sir Walter Raleigh were fresh in the minds of everyone. Most persons who had lived in or gone down to London before the theaters were closed in 1642 had visited the Globe Theatre and had seen, among others, the plays of Kit Marlowe, Ben Jonson, and Will Shakespeare. Sir Francis Bacon, in the spirit of the Renaissance, had "taken all knowledge to be his province." The expanding horizons were both geographical and intellectual. In spite of political intrigue and the bloody Tower of London, where Sir Walter Raleigh eventually languished, this had been the reign of the Good Queen Bess, the reign under which most of our first immigrants had been born.

The intellectual impact of this background upon Anne Bradstreet was profound. Though Elizabeth had died before Anne was born and Raleigh while she was still a small child, her adoration of Queen Elizabeth's image and her imitation of Sir Walter Raleigh's history are positive evidence that these were familiar names in her household. It is quite possible, too, that young Anne had seen a play or two since, as shall be shown hereafter, she was familiar with Shakespeare.

In the Earl of Lincoln's household Dudley and his daughter Anne must have had unrestricted access to an excellent library. Dudley, "a magazine of history,"[4] encouraged his daughter in her reading and education. Also, distinguished people moved in the society of the Earl of Lincoln, particularly those who, in the crucial years, looked with growing dissatisfaction at the highhandedness of Charles I and the vindictive intolerance of Archbishop Laud. Some of these, as well as the Dudleys and Anne's new husband, Simon Bradstreet, signed the patent in 1629 to remove themselves to America.

Most of the men who joined the group were graduates of Oxford or Cambridge. Simon himself had bachelor's and master's degrees. Dudley had had a broad education in the world of war, politics, and administration. It was not likely that such men as these would leave their cultural training behind them even though their future homes would bear little resemblance to the Earl's drawing room. The most precious possessions they took with them were their books. It is not surprising, therefore, to find the Dudleys and Bradstreets with libraries in their new homes. It would be fortunate for our study of influences on the poet if we could refer to lists of books contained in their libraries and that of the Earl of Lincoln. Unfortunately, we cannot. The Earl's library has long since been scattered. There is only a small and incomplete list of Dudley's books[5] left at his death; and none of these, except for Camden's histories, which Anne mentions in her "Four Monarchies" and which she may very well *not* have read, has any relationship to her poems.

Most tragic of all was the loss by fire of a fairly large

library belonging to the Bradstreets. Their son Simon recorded in his diary: "July 12, 1666. Whilst I was at N. London my fathers house at Andover was burnt, where I lost my books. . . . Tho: my own losse of books (and papers espec.) was great and my fathers far more being about 800, yet ye Lord was pleased gratiously many wayes to make up the same to us." However, we really do not need specific evidence of books with which Anne Bradstreet came in contact because her poetry is rich with direct or indirect references and influences. Their presence comes through to show the wide range of her reading and thinking.

Specific details of her life in New England are more elusive. There is no portrait of Anne Bradstreet, no marker left to indicate the whereabouts of her grave, no Bradstreet house left standing[6] nor its location certain, no contemporary characterization except in the commendatory poems and the letter to the reader from her brother-in-law in the first edition and in a funeral elegy appended to the second edition. So little evidence! Yet from her poetry emerges a distinct and charming personality the reader cannot forget. She was a Puritan woman whose early life in physical and intellectual luxury was in direct conflict with the primitive life of the New World. How she reconciled these differences and how she grew both spiritually and as a poet are the subjects of this study.

Her development in both respects came somewhat late. She was thirty-eight when *The Tenth Muse* appeared, and it contained, with some exceptions, the poetry least likely to give her enduring fame. The "four times four" long poems on the elements, man's humors, the ages of man, and the seasons, and also "The Four Monarchies" are the work of a novice. The other poems in the first edition have some intrinsic interest, to be discussed later, but structurally they are the work of an amateur.

The poems added to the second (posthumous) edition of 1678, many dated after 1650, and the prose added to the fourth (Ellis) edition of 1867 are markedly different in content, structure, and attitudes. They show a fine maturation of spiritual and poetic growth. It is with these differences in mind that the early and later periods are examined to discover the road of the Christian pilgrim carrying her burden of doubt and rebellion to ultimate reconciliation and the path of the poet from wooden imitation to true lyric expression.

He who reads her book will find the path of the Christian pilgrim and the path of the poet mounting steadily upward in its pages, for there, to paraphrase her own words, he may find what was the living author's mind.

CHAPTER 2

The Christian Pilgrimage

THE LONG POEMS contained in *The Tenth Muse* are reflections and imitations of Anne Bradstreet's favorite poets. The reader can plow his weary way through some two hundred pages of rhyming couplets written in the manner of the seventeenth-century favorite, Guillaume de Salluste, Sieur Du Bartas, or echoing other writers whom she had read, notably Sir Walter Raleigh, whom she paraphrased in "The Four Monarchies." The reader can plow his weary way and then lay the book down firmly and permanently with the conclusion that historically it is an interesting phenomenon: the work of the first woman—in fact, the first poet—in America to have a volume of verse published; but beyond that, he may conclude, there is nothing. Such, in fact, has been the estimate of many readers who leafed too casually through the book.

I *The Trials*

However, for others there is another estimate; for in this work, so patently imitative, is sublimated the spirit of a rebellious woman who wrote during the period of her greatest trial. Afterward, in retrospect, she could tell her children how her heart rose against her new circumstances and how she sometimes questioned the truth of spiritual matters accepted by her religious sect. She endured many hardships that would indeed make the heart and the mind of an intelligent woman rebellious and skeptical. Taken from a home of luxury and put down in a wilderness, she had imposed upon her a terrible adjustment. It is no wonder that she questioned the wisdom of the Puritans' removal to America and even the beliefs that motivated it. Moreover, she endured wretched health; and during the first few years of her residence in the colony she suffered the disappointment of not having children. Her own words to her children tell her story best:

> After a short time I changed my condition and was married, and came into this country, where I found a new world and new manners, at which my heart rose. But after I was convinced it was the way of God, I submitted to it and joined to the church at Boston.
>
> After some time I fell into a lingering sicknes like a consumption, together with a lamenesse, which correction I saw the Lord sent to humble and try me and doe mee Good: and it was not altogether ineffectuall.
>
> It pleased God to keep me a long time without a child, which was a great greif to me, and cost mee many prayers and tears before I obtaind one. . . .

With these terrible disappointments came the trials of religious doubting, the natural product of an intelligent mind:

> I have often been perplexed that I have not found that constant Joy in my Pilgrimage and refreshing which I supposed most of the servants of God have. . . . Yet have I many Times sinkings and droopings, and not enjoyed that felicity that sometimes I have done. But when I have been in darknes and seen no light, yet have I desired to stay my self upon the Lord. . . .
>
> Many times hath Satan troubled me concerning the verity of the scriptures, many times by Atheisme how I could know whether there was a God; I never saw any miracles to confirm me, and those which I read of how did I know but they were feigned.

Then, anticipating eighteenth-century thought,* she continues: "That there is a God my Reason would soon tell me by the wondrous workes that I see, the vast frame of the Heaven and the Earth, the order of all things. . . ." There were other doubts that beset her: "Why may not the Popish Religion bee the right? They have the same God, the same Christ, the same word: They only enterprett it one way, wee another." She even questioned, "Is there ffaith upon earth? and I have not known what to think."[1]

In his prize-winning poem, "Homage to Mistress Bradstreet," John Berryman sees very clearly the soul struggle of this Puritan woman:

> John Cotton shines on Boston's sin—
> I am drawn, in pieties that seem
> The weary drizzle of an unremembered dream.
> Women have gone mad
> at twenty-one
>
> I must be disciplined,
> in arms, against that one, and our
>   dissidents, and myself.[2]

She must be disciplined against the worldly temptations of Satan, against those who are openly rebellious—Anne Hutchinson? Roger Williams?—against herself who questions too much the hardships of this life, even of life itself, and the thinking of her fellow creatures.

To rebel, as Anne Hutchinson had done, was unthinkable. Neither her health nor her temperament, and certainly not her position as the wife and daughter of politically and socially prominent administrators of Massachusetts Bay, would permit it. She walked circumspectly in the path of righteousness, as was to be expected of a Puritan woman. Anne Bradstreet was not being hypocritical, for her abiding

---

* The eighteenth century, which emphasized knowledge derived from reason and the intellect rather than from intuitive perception, saw the world as an ordered universe created by a divine intelligence.

faith in her own personal God was deep, and it was the chief aid in her ultimate reconciliation of the world and the spirit. Meanwhile, the conflict was real. For Anne Hutchinson, rebellion was open and active; for Anne Bradstreet, emotions found their outlet in her domestic duties and in the self-imposed task of writing long poems in the manner of recent poets whom she admired.

II *Adam's Fall*

What would be more appropriate for her Puritan world than to imitate Du Bartas' *La Premier Semaine* (1578), translated by Joshua Sylvester, and Sir Walter Raleigh's *History of the World* (1614)? The first gave an account of the creation; the second began with it. The subject matter of these two authors was of vital interest to the Puritans, whose doctrine was based upon the story of Adam's fall and whose reading of history was not to satisfy an interest in the humanities but to find moral lessons to be derived from the behavior of men in the past. In fact, the purpose of most Puritan writing was didactic, whether it was sermon, history, or poetry. Louis B. Wright explains the importance of such writers as Du Bartas and Raleigh to the Puritans:

> An important reason for popularity on both sides of the Atlantic of Du Bartas' versified description of the creation in his *Divine Weeks and Works* was the encyclopedic information it contained. While Anne Bradstreet was absorbing enough poetic inspiration from Du Bartas to make her the Tenth Muse, many a less exalted reader was acquiring from the same source information which he accepted as scientific truth about God's universe. . . .

Mr. Wright continues his analysis of Anne Bradstreet's favorite, Sir Walter Raleigh's *History of the World*: "Favored by the Puritans because it demonstrated the divine purpose in human events. . . . Most readers would have agreed with

Raleigh's preparatory statement that 'wee may gather out of History a policy no lesse wise than eternall; by comparison and application of other mens forepassed miserie's with our own like errours & ill deservings'. . . . The colonists, like their kindred in England, read Raleigh's *History* not merely as a compendium of facts about the ancient world, but also as a source of political and moral truths."[3]

Moralizing on the punishment of Nebuchadnezzar, which he has just recounted, Raleigh says:

> All humane affections, wherein due reference to God is wanting, are no better than obscure clouds, hindring the influence of that blessed light, which clarifies the soule of man, and predisposeth it unto the brightnesse of eternall felicity; so that insolent joy, which man in the pride of his vaine imagination conceiveth of his own worth, doth above all other passions blast our mindes, as it were with lightning, & makes us to reflect our thoughts upon our seeming inherent greatnesse, forgetting the whilest him, to whom we are indebted for our very being.[4]

Another example of Raleigh's moralizing is the conclusion to his book on the Persian government: "Such was the Tyrannicall condition of the *Persian* Government; and such are generally the effects of Luxury, when it is joyned with absolute power."[5]

In her parallel history of the Persian government, Anne Bradstreet refers to Raleigh in the short concluding verse to this chapter of history.[6] Again and again she mentions him by name. John Harvard Ellis, in his able introduction to the 1867 edition of her poems, shows with numerous examples that she frequently paraphrased Raleigh in her "Four Monarchies."

Recognizing unmistakable parallels between the poem and the history, we turn with confidence, especially with the times of the poet in our minds, to discover parallels in the statements of moral truths. To our astonishment, we find practically none. Occasionally, she implies a moral in a rather effective concise statement: Of Belshazzar she wrote: "His lust and crueltyes in storyes find,/A royal State rul'd by a bruitish mind."[7] Of Alexander: "His temperance is but a sordid thing,/No wayes becoming such a mighty King."[8] Of Belus: "But yet this blot forever on him lies,/He taught the people first to Idolize."[9]

Truths could be learned by the reader from these commentaries, yet they are disposed of in two brief lines. Moreover, they deal with the conduct of particular people and are not expanded into the moral lessons for which Raleigh had set an example. The suspicion of the poet's indifference or purposeful neglect of such sermons, as would please her audience even more than would Raleigh's, is further strengthened by the fact that she included no preface like Raleigh's to declare a high moral purpose in writing her history.

Moreover, in the first edition of her work there is a surprising infrequency of comment or reference to the subjects dearest to the Puritan heart: the fall of Adam, the inheritance of his sin, and the doctrine of the elect. Her reference to "Adams Race" in the dedication to her father is not only incidental but almost flippant:

> Dear Sir of late delighted with the sight
> Of your four Sisters cloth'd in black and white,
> Of fairer Dames the Sun, ne'r saw the face;
> Though made a pedestal for *Adams* Race. . . .[10]

In her "Four Ages of Man," she is reminded of Adam in her portrait of "Childhood." Her eight beloved children could not have been pious little Puritans all the time; now and then they must have seemed, indeed, the children of Adam. While this remark may be taken to be facetious, nevertheless the characteristics of childhood, bad as well as good, are portrayed too realistically by Anne not to have come from her experience rather than from biblical concepts. Childhood says,

The sins and dangers I am subject to,
Stained from birth with *Adams* sinfull fact,
Thence I began to sin as soon as act;
A perverse will, a love to what's forbid,
A serpents sting in pleasing face lay hid . . .[11]

There is one other reference by Childhood to original sin,
when he begins his speech with: "Ah me! conceiv'd in sin
and born with sorrow . . ."[12]

Aside from these references, we search in vain among the
poems of the first edition for explicit poetic discussion of
this basic premise of Puritan theology. Indeed the most
striking omission is the "history" of man's creation and fall.
Both Du Bartas and Raleigh begin their stories with the
creation, as was the custom among many writers of history.
The chapter of greatest significance to the Puritans, of course,
was the first one; their own sermons, diaries, and journals
were permeated, directly or indirectly, with this theme. Yet
Anne Bradstreet not only makes comparatively few references
to Adam's fall or to the doctrine of election;* she begins
her "History of the Four Monarchies" not with the creation
but with the Assyrian Monarchy. It may be objected that
had she introduced these themes in the beginning or con-
tinued her history into the Christian era, where election
might very well have been discussed, her poetic scheme of
sets of four poems dealing only with monarchies would have
been disrupted. Moreover, she begins her history where Du
Bartas left his at his death. She had found "*Bartas* sugar'd
lines"[13] dazzling her sight; she "honored him but would not
wear his wealth."[14] Perhaps this could be taken to mean
that she felt so humble in reading his poetry that she dared
not tamper with the same subject.

These suppositions could be true, but it is hardly likely
that a devout woman wholly given to the cause of Puritanism
would neglect writing on a subject so fundamental to her

* See Introduction, pp. 20ff.

fellow Puritans. An introductory poem on man's inheritance from Adam could very well have paved the way for the stories of wicked men of history. But Anne Bradstreet does not dwell at length on the wickedness of man, originally or historically.

In the first edition of her work, there is also a significant omission of typical Puritan moralizing. Does this not seem strange at a time when many Puritans were busy hammering upon the twin themes of Adam's fall and election, at a time when the fear of God as an angry ruler was made no less convincing by the difficult and trying circumstances under which they were living?

There can be only one conclusion: she was writing during the period of doubt and questioning she so eloquently described at a later date to her children, and she was doggedly writing her long poems of rhyming couplets not just out of a natural poetic impulse but to find an outlet[15] for a pent-up rebellion against a new world forced upon her and against the Puritan "pieties that seemed the weary drizzle of an unremembered dream." A woman less resourceful might indeed "have gone mad at twenty-one."

For her, in the first twenty years of her life in America, there could be only one conclusion: all is vanity. It is appropriate that the first edition of Anne Bradstreet's poems should end with "Of the Vanity of all worldly creatures." Even though it seems at times a mere paraphrase of Ecclesiastes, whose author's questioning spirit was so attuned to her own, it must be the sincere cry of this tortured woman.

> As he said vanity, so vain say I,
> Oh! vanity, O vain all under sky;
> Where is the man can say, lo I have found
> On brittle Earth, a Consolation sound?[16]

Like the other author, she looks about her and sees all man's endeavors are in vain. But unlike him, she has faith that she will find the *Summum Bonum*.

This pearl of price, this tree of life, this spring
Who is possessed of, shall reign a King.
Nor change of state, nor cares shall ever see,
But wear his crown unto eternity:
This satiates the Soul, this stayes the mind,
And all the rest, but Vanity, we find.[17]

With the exception of this revealing piece on "The Vanity
of All Worldly Creatures," the rest of the poems of the first
edition give no outward evidence of the poet's inward struggle
because they were written impersonally and objectively. It
is only through this example and her later confession that
we have been able to probe beneath the surface of her
earlier work.

III   *The Battle Won*

The letter to her children containing the confession of her
earlier spiritual struggle and rebellion introduced a manuscript
volume of poems carefully transcribed from the original by
her son, the Reverend Simon Bradstreet. This was "kept as
a precious relic by her descendants" until John Harvard Ellis
included them in his (the fourth) edition of her work. He
included also some pieces, "Meditations Divine and Morall,"
from an original manuscript written for Simon, at his request,
but unfinished at the time of Anne's death. Other less deeply
personal poems had been added to the second edition of 1678.

The evidence that most, if not all, of these additions were
written later than *The Tenth Muse* is not only that many
are dated after its publication—some as late as the 1660's.
Of greater significance is the fact that their author had not
only kicked the traces of the rhyming pentameter couplet
and slavish imitation but had also gained spiritual confidence.

Seeing her first work in print had brought the truth home
to her. It was "an ill-form'd offspring" . . . a "rambling brat
in print."[18] Henceforward, she would write poetry not from
others' writings but out of her own experiences, in lyrics, as

they should be. These poems were so personal that she saved them for her children for the time when she would be no more with them, not only that they might have a "dayly remembrance" but that they might "gain some spiritual Advantage" from these records of her experiences. "I have not studied in this you read to show my skill, but to declare the Truth—not to sett forth myself, but the Glory of God."[19]

The truth and the glory of God were now manifest as she put the poems together for her children. They are an autobiographical record of her onslaughts of fever and "fainting fitts," from each of which she was sure she had been rescued in answer to her prayers. Illness, prayer, recovery—this was the pattern throughout this part of her life. She wept and prayed, sometimes in an agony of suffering; a few times she doubted; but, released of suffering, she could compose her hymn of praise and thanksgiving. A cynic might say that the hymn came after the fact, not before or during her agony. But to Anne Bradstreet, the recovery was simply the answer of God, who had heard and understood. It was not even a miracle.

> I sought him whom my Soul did Love,
> With tears I sought him earnestly;
> He bow'd his ear down from Above,
> In vain I did not seek or cry.[20]

The record of her physical and spiritual suffering, realistically told, made a stronger testimony to God's compassion when she was released.

> When Sorrowes had begyrt me round,
>   And Paines within and out,
> When in my flesh no part was found,
>   Then didst thou rid me out.
>
> My burning flesh in sweat did boyle,
>   My aking head did break;
> From side to side for ease I toyle,
>   So faint I could not speak.

Beclouded was my Soul with fear
   Of thy Displeasure sore,
Nor could I read my Evidence
   Which oft I read before.

Hide not thy face from me, I cry'd,
   From Burnings keep my soul;
Thou know'st my heart, and hast me try'd;
   I on thy Mercyes Rowl.

O, heal my Soul, thou know'st I said,
   Tho' flesh consume to nought;
What tho' in dust it shall bee lay'd,
   To Glory't shall bee brought.

Thou heardst, thy rod thou didst remove,
   And spar'd my Body frail,
Thou shew'st to me thy tender Love,
   My heart no more might quail.

O, Praises to my mighty God,
   Praise to my Lord, I say,
Who hath redeem'd my Soul from pitt:
   Praises to him for Aye![21]

This poem is unusual in one respect: in none of her other writings do we smell the sulphurous fumes of Hell. We do not feel that hers was the avenging God of the Puritans, the one soon to be made terrifying in the Reverend Michael Wiggleworth's *The Day of Doom*. Rather the idea of divine and tender love predominates throughout Anne Bradstreet's poems.

IV *Vengeful God*

Like the other Puritans, however, she felt that illness and misfortune were visited upon God's creatures for their own waywardness. In retrospect, she knew that when she was "14 or 15" she had found her heart "more carnall, and sitting loose from God," for "vanity and the follyes of youth" had taken hold of her. The next year the Lord "smott" her with smallpox.

In the letter to her children, she would say,

> If at any time you are chastened of God, take it as thankfully and Joyfully as in greatest mercyes, for if yee bee his yee shall reap the greatest benefitt by it. It hath been no small support to me in times of Darknes when the Almighty hath hid his face from me, that yet I have had abundance of sweetnes and refreshment after affliction, and more circumspection in my walking after I have been afflicted. I have been with God like an untoward child, that no longer then the rod has been on my back (or at least in sight) but I have been apt to forgett him and myself too. Before I was afflicted I went astray, but now I keep thy statutes.[22]

She had been "like an untoward child." She had, in her own mind, "gone astray" in those early years of doubt; but at last, after so many trials and so much chastening from God, her faith was secure and the ways of God accepted.

Toward the end of her life, she wrote "Meditations Divine and morall" for her son Simon. They were, as their title suggests, didactic pieces, and they were also unlike anything she had written before. Life, however difficult, had taught her a great deal. No longer rebellious, she could write out of her wisdom the lessons to be learned in man's world and in the larger world about him.

V *Puritan Poet*

In great measure, she had even learned to accept some basic tenets of Puritanism. In these meditations and in some of her other late work she showed the influence of the Puritan world of which she had at last become a part. Some of its ideas which she reflects are:

1. Every fact of life has spiritual meaning: "There is no object that we see; no action that we doe; no good that we

injoy; no evil that we feele, or fear, but we may make some spirituall advantage of all: and he that makes such improvment is wise, as well as pious."[23]

2. God has made men unequal in body and mind. Upon this basic principle, the Puritans had concluded that some, like themselves, were the only ones fit to rule; the rest were made to be ruled: "There is nothing admits of more admiration, then Gods various dispensation of his gifts among the sons of men, betwixt whom he hath put so vast a disproportion that they scarcly seem made of the same lump, or sprung out of the loynes of one Adam; some set in the highest dignity that mortality is capable off; and some again so base, that they are viler then the earth . . . and no other reason can be given of all this, but so it pleased him, whose will is the perfect rule of righteousnesse."[24]

3. God can and does take part in the affairs of man. This concept is shown in her prayers to God to give her husband not only a safe journey in affairs abroad but a successful transaction of business. Both prayers being answered, she composes a poem of praise and thanksgiving.

4. There is one Christ at the head of a hierarchy of souls: ". . . in the church both militant and triumphant, there is but one Christ, who is the Sun of righteousnes, in the midest of an innumerable company of Saints and Angels; those Saintes have their degrees even in this life, some are Stars of the first magnitude, and some of a lesse degree; and others (and they indeed the most in number), but small and obscure, yet all receive their luster (be it more or lesse) from that glorious sun that inlightens all in all; . . ."[25]

5. God has decreed election and reprobation: "All the works and doings of God are wonderfull, but none more awfull than his great worke of election and Reprobation."[26]

None more "awfull than . . . election and Reprobation"—did she entirely accept the last tenet? There is precious little—as we have noted—in any of her work, early or late, about Adam's fall, man's inherited sin, and the doctrine of election and reprobation. With rare exceptions, her eyes were on heaven. God's ways on earth might be inscrutable, but they must be accepted, even in the midst of suffering, as the way of a loving not an angry God. On August 28, 1656, she wrote:

> After much weaknes and sicknes when my spirits were worn out, and many times my faith weak likewise, the Lord was pleased to uphold my drooping heart, and to manifest his Love to me; and this is that which stayes my Soul that this condition that I am in is the best for me, for God doth not afflict willingly, nor take delight in greiving the children of men: he hath no benefitt by my adversity, nor is he the better for my prosperity; but he doth it for my Advantage, and that I may bee a Gainer by it. And if he knowes that weaknes and a frail body is the best to make me a vessell fitt for his use, why should I not bare it, not only willingly but joyfully? The Lord knowes I dare not desire that health that somtimes I have had, least my heart should bee drawn from him, and sett upon the world.

> Now I can wait, looking every day when my Saviour shall call for me. Lord graunt that while I live I may doe that service I am able in this frail Body, and bee in continuall expectation of my change, and let me never forgett thy great Love to my soul so lately expressed, when I could lye down and bequeath my Soul to thee, and Death seem'd no terrible Thing. O let me ever see Thee that Art invisible, and I shall not bee unwilling to come, tho: by so rough a Messenger.[27]

She lived to be sixty, a remarkable age considering the ruggedness of the times and the weakness of her body. Toward the end of her life, three years before her death, the weary pilgrim longed to be at rest and to "soare on high among the blest."

> As weary pilgrim, now at rest,
>   Hugs with delight his silent nest

His wasted limbes, now lye full soft
   That myrie steps, have troden oft
Blesses himself, to think upon
   his dangers past, and travailes done
The burning sun no more shall heat
   Nor stormy raines, on him shall beat.
. . . .

A pilgrim I, on earth, perplext
   with sinns with cares and sorrows vext
By age and paines brought to decay
   and my Clay house mouldring away
Oh how I long to be at rest
   and soare on high among the blest.
This body shall in silence sleep
   Mine eyes no more shall ever weep
No fainting fits shall me assaile
   nor grinding paines my body fraile
. . . .

A Corrupt Carcasse downe it lyes
   a glorious body it shall rise
In weaknes and dishonour sowne
   in power 'tis rais'd by Christ alone
Then soule and body shall unite
   and of their maker have the sight
Such lasting joyes shall there behold
   as eare ne'r heard nor tongue e'er told
Lord make me ready for that day
   then Come deare bridgrome Come away.[28]

The weary pilgrim had traveled far. At last, as she came
to the end of her journey, doubts had vanished and her
faith was secure.

CHAPTER 3

The Apprentice

L IKE THAT OF THE PILGRIM, the path of the poet led
steadily upward: from rebellion to assurance, from im-
maturity to maturity.

Critics since Anne Bradstreet's time have failed to share the
enthusiasm manifested by her contemporaries for her first
volume of poetry. The long, painful quaternions in imitation
of Du Bartas, and the elegy in his honor, have been condemned for their laboring couplets: "On the whole these
poems are tedious, unleavened by imaginative power, and
cramped by diction. She never mastered the pentameter
couplet."[1] "The painstaking elaboration of the 'quaternions'
interests the modern reader only as survivals of medieval
jugglery."[2]

Yet she is sometimes charitably excused because Du Bartas,
whose poetic lines are as laborious as her own, was universally
admired by famous writers of the seventeenth century, even
by so eminent a poet and critic as Dryden. With some condescension, the modern reader skims over or skips the five
long poems and finds his real pleasure in those added
posthumously to the second and fourth editions of her work.
It would seem worth our while, however, to probe further
into the early poems, since they show the poet's wide interests:
in ancient and contemporary science and medicine, in politics
and social problems at home and abroad, in history, and in
women. In some poems, also, like "The Four Ages of Man"
and "The Four Seasons," there is something more than

stilted pentameter lines. They are poems influenced by her own observations, anticipating her later work.

She relates the first three of her quaternions to the Hippocratic and Aristotelian scheme of things, with her own variations:

Elements:	Water (wet and cold)	Air (moist and hot)	Fire (hot and dry)	Earth (cold and dry)
Humours:	Flegm (unstable)	Blood (sanguine)	Black bile (choleric)	Yellow bile (spleen) (melancholic)
Ages:	Childhood	Youth (spring)	Middle age (summer)	Old age (autumn, winter)

Childhood is the child of flegm and the grandchild of water; youth, the child of blood and grandchild of air, *et cetera*.

These groups—the elements, the humours, and the ages of man—together with another group, "The Four Seasons" form her "four times four" quaternions. All sixteen parts are personified like characters of a morality play as they take their places upon the stage.[3] "Their method was . . ./That each should tel, what of himselfe he knew;/Both good and bad, but yet no more then's true."[4]

I *"The Four Elements"*

But, like so many human beings, each of the elements and the humours, at least, is chiefly interested in telling how he "was the strongest, noblest and the best," puffing up his own virtues, if necessary, at the expense of the others. Indeed, the arguments become more and more heated until, among the humours, they are vituperative. The elements had good intentions that were soon forgotten:

> Who the most good could shew, & who most rage
> For to declare, themselves they all ingage;
> And in due order each her turne should speake,

> But enmity, this amity did breake:
> All would be cheife, and all scorn'd to be under,
> Whence issu'd raines, and winds, lightning and
> thunder . . .[5]

Though the elements are personified, their characteristics are, in the true sense, natural. While beneficial to man, each can, if unrestrained, cause his destruction. Fire can turn a town to cinders; Earth, though productive, can bring famine and earthquake; Water, by its abundance or lack of it, can bring benefits or disaster; Air is the breath of every living thing without which it perishes. Each Element argues his power and his superiority, and he shows that none of the other three can get along without him.

II *"The Four Humours"*

The arguments of these four are not so heated, however, as their author's introductory remarks would lead us to believe. In fact, most of what they say is true; their fault lies in that each wishes to be chief. It is with some shock, therefore, particularly considering the poet's usually gentle manner, that we discover the splenetic language contained in "The Four Humours," in which each wishes to be paramount even if he has to slander the others to do so.[6] Their arguments have the tone of political backbiting. There seems to be something more than the mere personification of man's humours. To be sure, there is one reasonable explanation: the analysis of the four humours gives Anne Bradstreet a beautiful opportunity to dwell on her favorite subject of anatomy. By the time we have finished reading this quaternion, we have almost finished a course in the subject. Even so, this does not explain the atmosphere of violence and hatred; so we finish reading "The Four Humours" with the suspicion that here is more than meets the eye.

It would be a neat trick if we could establish the fact that

Anne Bradstreet had certain episodes or certain persons in mind as she wrote it, and it is possible she had. Considering her own rebellion and her own doubts of orthodoxy, she might have felt some sympathy for Roger Williams, banished in 1636, and certainly for Anne Hutchinson, exiled in 1637. During that time Dudley was deputy governor of Massachusetts and sat at the trial. Anne Bradstreet's husband was an administrative assistant in the governor's office. To have spoken out against the treatment of the two "heretics" would have been dangerous for anyone; for the governor's daughter, it would have brought disgrace upon the whole family. There are other possibilities, too, for the colony, in spite of its Christian brotherhood, was in frequent turmoil, politically and theologically.

The portrayal of Choler as irascible would be a faithful image, but in this poem he is given to unusually nasty remarks about his brother humours. They are all "milksops." Blood, "while worth the other two," is "Sister Ruddy":

> That much wil talk, but little dares she do,
> Unlesse to court, and claw, and dice, and drink,
> And there she wil out-bid us all, I think . . .
>
> . . . .
>
> She loves her sword, only because its gilt.

Is this the portrait of a British or colonial contemporary? And then there is Melancholy, whom Choler disposes of with equal scorn:

> Then here's our sad black Sister, worse then you,
> She'l neither say, she wil, nor wil she doe:
> But peevish, Male-content, musing she sits,
> And by misprisions, like to loose her wits; . . .

"Misprision" is by definition the neglect of duty by a public official. A public official of New England? England? And then there is Flegme, seen through the eyes of Choler:

> So loving unto all, she scornes to fight.
> If any threaten her, she'l in a trice,
> Convert from water, to congealed Ice . . .
>
> .   .   .   .
>
> She dare, not challenge if I speake amisse;
> Nor hath she wit, or heat, to blush at this.

A contemporary sycophant?

Choler has not finished his derogatory characterizations. He launches into a long anatomical analysis showing how all the other humours, with their "seats" in the human system, cannot function without him (heat): "Take Choler from a Prince, what is he more,/Then a dead Lyon? . . ." (One suspects a bit of Anne Bradstreet's sly humor here.) For Melancholy, with his seat in the spleen, Choler has the lowest opinion: "So base thou art, that baser cannot be;/The excrement, adustion of me."[7]

Melancholy does not forget this insult. Biding her time until Blood has refuted the slanderous remarks about her and has established her rightful place of importance, Melancholy launches forth in a diatribe against Choler that would shock to attention a reader gone to sleep over poetic analyses of anatomy:

> Thou do'st assume my name, wel be it just;
> This transmutation is, but not excretion,
> Thou wants Philosophy, and yet discretion.
> Now by your leave, Ile let your greatnesse see;
> What officer thou art to al us three.
> The Kitchin Drudge, the cleanser of the sinks,
> That casts out all that man or eates, or drinks.
> Thy bittering quality, stil irretates,
> Til filth and thee, nature exhonorates.
> If any doubt this truth, whence this should come;
> Show them thy passage to the' *Duodenum.*[8]

What caused the poet to write in this surprising manner? The explanation that she was merely following her interests in anatomy or recording the usual concepts of man's humours and their origins is not enough. In none of the other portrayals does she indulge in anything so elemental, so unlike the usual, deceptively proper tone of her poetry. We have been aware of her spiritual rebellion. We suspect that she was also sick of bickerings, political as well as religious, among her fellowmen.

Flegme closes the arguments of "The Four Humours." She claims for herself the noblest parts of man, the Brain and the Soul. She argues with a sweet reasonableness appropriate to both, and she concludes with an interesting turn of thought: she asks them to settle their differences and work together in harmony, for otherwise all will fall into confusion. And she concludes with a call to Unity spelled in italicized letters:

> Let's now be friends, 'tis time our spight was spent,
> Lest we too late, this rashnesse do repent,
> Such premises wil force a sad conclusion,
> Unlesse we 'gree, all fals into confusion.
> Let Sanguine, Choler, with her hot hand hold,
> To take her moyst, my moistnesse wil be bold;
> My cold, cold Melanchollies hand shal clasp,
> Her dry, dry Cholers other hand shal grasp;
> Two hot, two moist, two cold, two dry here be,
> A golden Ring, the Posey, *Unity* . . .[9]

Only when each is tempered or modified by the rest, only when all understand each other, can Unity be established. Was this a plea to the poet's wrangling contemporaries?

Almost from their arrival in 1630, the colonists had been in a turmoil about something, when not about the French and Indians, then among themselves. Regardless of his ideas, which seem to us now liberal and right, wherever Roger Williams went there was trouble—first in Plymouth, then in Salem. Even John Endicott was to learn this to his sorrow when Williams persuaded him to cut the cross from the king's colors as "being a relique of antichristian superstition."

Mr. Williams was banished; Mr. Endicott deprived of his license, so to speak, to hold office for a year.

Henry Vane—young, charming, inexperienced, bull-headed —was sent from England to become governor, a fact resented by many of the colonists who favored Deputy Governor Winthrop. It was not the time for inexperience. The colony was in an uproar about Antinomianism, and Mr. Wheelwright was brought before a court for preaching the same heresies as his sister-in-law, Anne Hutchinson. Both were soon to be banished, but court action on Wheelwright was postponed because of trouble with the Pequods, who were presently to be destroyed by the colonists (with assistance from the Narragansetts). Then, once more, internal dissensions began:

Towards the end of the year, religious heats became more violent, and the civil affairs more sensibly affected by them. The people of Boston in general were in favour of Mr. Vane the governor, the rest of the towns in general for Mr. Winthrop the deputy governor. At a sessions of the court in March, it was moved that the court of elections for 1637 should not be held in Boston, but in Newtown (Cambridge.) Nothing could be more mortifying to the governor; and as he could not hinder the vote by a negative, he refused to put the question. Mr. Winthrop the deputy governor, as he lived in Boston, excused himself, and the court required Mr. Endicot, one of the assistants, to do it. It was carried for the removal.

. . . .

At the opening of the court of election for 1637, . . . a petition was again offered [a petition protesting the court's proceedings against Wheelwright] . . . which the governor, Mr. Vane, would have had read; but Mr. Winthrop, the deputy governor, opposed it as being out of order . . . after the elections were over, the petition might be read. The governor and those of his party would not proceed, unless the petition was read. The time being far spent, and many persons calling for election, the deputy governor called to the people to divide, and the greater number should carry it; which was done, and the majority was for proceeding. Still the governor refused until the deputy governor told him they would go on without him. This caused him to submit. Mr. Winthrop was chosen governor, Mr. Dudley deputy governor, Mr. Saltonstall, son of Sir Richard, and Mr. Stoughton new assistants; and Mr. Vane and his friends of the same persuasion, Dummer, Haugh and Coddington, left out of the magistry. There was great danger of a violent tummult that day. The speeches on both sides were fierce, and they began to lay hands on one another, but the manifest majority on one side was a restraint to the other. Boston waited the event of this election of magistrates before they would choose their representatives for the other business of the general court, and the next morning they chose Mr. Vane the late governor, Mr. Coddington and Mr. Haugh. This election of Boston was immediately determined by the court to be undue. . . . A warrant issued for a new choice, and Boston returned the same men again, and then they were not rejected . . . Mr. Vane professed himself ready to serve the cause of God in the meanest capacity. He was notwithstanding much mortified. . . .[10]

In 1637 occurred also the trial, excommunication, and banishment of Anne Hutchinson. Her contemporary, the other Anne, was as much aware as everybody else of the trial, the court's hostile questions, and the defendant's cool, uncompromising even defiant answers, which frustrated the judges even in her "recantation." The whole procedure must have been discussed in the homes of the Dudleys and the Bradstreets. Anne Bradstreet who probably even then was wondering whether the Popish religion might not have been right—recognizing that it had the same God, the same Christ, the same word as the Protestant Puritans, the only difference being in interpretation—must have listened with sympathy to the story of another who interpreted church doctrine differently from the accepted beliefs of other church members. It surely would have grieved and offended her to learn the words of the intolerant Hooker's pronouncement against Mrs. Hutchinson:

> The expression of providence against this wretched woman hath proceeded from the Lord's miraculous mercy, and his bare arm hath been discovered therein from first to last, that all the churches may hear and fear. I do believe such a heap of hideous errors at once to be vented by such a self-deluding and deluded creature, no history can record; and yet, after recantation of all, to be cast out as unsavoury salt, that she may not continue a pest to the place, that will be forever marvellous in the eyes of all the saints.[11]

The ultimate tragedy of Anne Hutchinson may have had its impact upon Anne Bradstreet's dissatisfactions. The suggestion that she was thinking of any or all of these people and events of contemporary history is admittedly tenuous; yet the wrangling in political circles and the intolerance of the godly seem the reflections of men in their "humours." One wonders whether "The Four Humours in Mans Constitution" was not tongue-in-cheek, a covert outlet for the poet's inward protest against man's inhumanity to man and a call for *Unity* "Lest we too late this rashness do repent. . . . Unless we agree, all falls into confusion."

Presumably the laborious task of composing "The Four Monarchies" came after the writing of "The Four Humours," for it was unfinished when the manuscript went to the publisher. It is reasonable to assume that Anne Bradstreet wrote in the same sequence as that of publication as she had made a careful and grand plan of her "four times four" poems. "The Four Humours" appears, as it logically should, after the first poem, "The Four Elements," since the former were "children" of the latter. This fact places their composition at an early date in the sequence, a date that may have been too early to make possible criticism of the crucial years in England in the dispute between Parliament and King Charles I, 1642-49. There were always, of course, the men about court who talked much but dared do little, who diced and drank, who neglected their duties as public officials, who had so little will to meet a crisis as to "turn in a thrice from water to congealed ice"—all characters to be found in "The Four Humours." However, it was not only the time of writing that makes reference in this poem to the crisis in England unlikely, but also the fact that its author chose to write boldly and openly about that crisis in her "Dialogue between Old England and New . . ." in 1642. She obviously felt no need to hide her feelings under cover of a poem like "The Four Humours." If, therefore, the latter is a covert criticism of contemporary events, it must be of New England.

Anne Bradstreet was definitely interested in the political scene, a fact that is not to be wondered at considering the position of her family in the Puritan community. It would be strange if current affairs, both at home and abroad, were not discussed in table conversation.

As Puritans, the people of Massachusetts maintained colonial government in a theocratic not a democratic system, limiting suffrage to church membership and office to those of superior talent supposedly chosen by God. Governor Winthrop had frankly recognized that the Creator had made some men superior to rule and others inferior to be ruled. In her later life Anne Bradstreet stated: "There is nothing admits of more admiration, then Gods various dispensation of his gifts among the sons of men, betwixt whom he hath put so vast a disproportion that they scarcly seem made of the same lump, or sprung out of the loynes of one Adam; . . ." God had not created men equal.

While the colonists maintained a Puritan theocratic government, they remained Englishmen under the sovereign of their native land. Political crises abroad disturbed these people at home. Like all Englishmen, they expressed their protests against political injustice, sometimes actively, as in the case against Governor Andros, sometimes in writing.

It is as an English Puritan woman that Anne Bradstreet looks with concern and sorrow at the crucial conflict between Charles I and Parliament in 1642. Ever since the arbitrary and vindictive power of Archbishop Laud, thinking laymen and clergy alike had felt there should be some curb on the autocratic power of churchmen in office. Reforms were proposed by a Committee on Religion, one of them recommending expulsion of bishops from the House of Lords, a measure passed by Commons and, after some delay, by the upper house. When Charles I, laying aside all the rights of constitutional monarchy, actually arrived himself with three hundred followers at the House of Commons to arrest for high treason the five offending members who were the prime movers of the reform, he found the foe absent and the remaining members in silence refusing to reveal their whereabouts. By this time all of Parliament was united against the king, and the people at large were becoming disaffected. Soon there was to be civil war.[12]

It is the approaching civil war that concerns Anne Bradstreet, and she voices her distress in "A Dialogue between Old England and New; concerning her present troubles, *Anno* 1642." Though she sympathizes with Parliament, her greatest fear is for the fate of her mother country.

New England, the daughter in the *Dialogue,* inquires of Old England, the mother, what is the cause of her woe. Old England sees the present conflict as a reflection of her unhappy past, of the fate of monarchs like Richard II, of the tragedy of the young princes and of Lady Jane, of the Wars of the Roses, and of Ireland's bloody chapter. These tragic scenes she remembers with a sense of guilt and sorrow:

> From crying bloods, yet cleansed am not I,
> Martyrs, and others, dying causelesly:
> How many Princely heads on blocks laid down,
> For nought, but title to a fading Crown?

She tells her daughter the cause of the present "grievance of her troubled Land"—

> Idolatry, supplanter of a Nation,
> With foolish superstitions adoration;
> And lik'd, and countenanc'd by men of might,
> The Gospel is trod down, and hath no right;
> Church Offices are sold, and bought, for gaine,
> That Pope, had hope, to find *Rome* here againe; . . .

And she reveals the conflict between Parliament and King—

> . . . there's grown of late,
> 'Twixt King and Peeres a question of state,
> Which is the chief, the law, or else the King,
> One saith its he, the other no such thing.
> My better part in Court of Parliament,
> To ease my groaning land shew their intent,
> To crush the proud, and right to each man deal.
> To help the Church, and stay the Common-Weal.
> . . . .
> Had they not held law fast, all had been gone.

She fears for the future:

> I that no warres, so many years have known,
> Am now destroy'd, and slaughter'd by mine own,
> But could the field alone this cause decide,
> One battell, two or three I might abide,
> But these may be beginnings of more woe,
> Who knows, the worst, the best may overthrow.

The daughter of Old England seems to comfort her mother with new hope by reminding her "that Right may have its right, though't be with blood," for was it not

> After dark Popery the day did clear,
> But now the Sun in's brightnesse shall appear,
> Blest be the Nobles of thy Noble Land,
> With (ventur'd lives) for truths defence that stand,

Blest be thy Commons, who for Common good,
And thine infringed Lawes have boldly stood.
Blest be thy Counties which do aid thee still

. . . .

These are the dayes, the Churches foes to crush,
To root out Prelates, head, tail, branch, and rush.

. . . .

Go on brave *Essex*, shew whose son thou art,
Not false to King, nor Countrey in thy heart,
But those that hurt his people and his Crown,
By force expell, destroy, and tread them down.
Let Gaoles be fill'd with th' remnant of that pack,
And sturdy *Tyburn* loaded till it crack . . .

. . . .

These, these, are they (I trust) with *Charles* our King,
Out of all mists, such glorious dayes will bring,
That dazzled eyes beholding much shall wonder
At that thy setled Peaee, thy wealth and splendour,
Thy Church and Weal, establish'd in such manner,
That all shall joy that thou display'dst thy banner,
And discipline erected, so I trust,
That nursing Kings, shall come and lick thy dust.[13]

,The poem ends in a burst of patriotic fervor, a vision of the
future of Old England in happiness and in peace, where Jew
and Gentile shall worship together and her name, fame, and
valor shall shine "As did thine Ancesturs [*sic*] in *Palestine*."

This is a poem by a patriotic English woman looking toward
the reunion of trustworthy nobles with their king and the
consequent return of Old England to the glory that is right-
fully hers. It is also the poem of a woman keenly aware of
contemporary events abroad and the close relationship between Old and New England. We may safely assume that
Anne Bradstreet was equally interested in affairs at home
and equally distressed at turmoil in her own political and
religious community. The one interest found expression in
a forthright call for loyalty and unity in "The Dialogue"; the

other, of necessity less outspoken, in the sometimes bitter portraits of "The Four Humours."

III *"The Four Ages of Man"*

"The Four Ages of Man," her third quaternion, has quite a different flavor. Its four characters do not behave in the manner of the elements or the "humours," although they are supposed to be the children of both. There is no contention for supremacy; each character tells his tale with frank admissions of his weaknesses as well as his strengths. However personified, these characters seem to be not mere abstractions but flesh and blood. We feel as if the author is dealing with childhood, youth, the manly, and old age in portraits of actual characters drawn from personal observation and experience.

Childhood's description of his mother's suffering can come only from the poet's own agony as she bore each of her first seven children—her agony and her great love.

My mothers breeding sicknes, I will spare;
Her nine months weary burden not declare.
To shew her bearing pangs, I should do wrong,
To tel that paine, which cann't be told by tongue;
With tears into this world I did arrive;
My mother stil did waste, as I did thrive:
Who yet with love, and all alacrity,
Spending was willing, to be spent for me;
With wayward cryes, I did disturbe her rest;
Who sought stil to appease me, with her brest,
With weary armes, she danc'd, and *By, By* sung, . . .

The writer's portrait of youth is less personal than that of childhood. It includes all youth, both good and bad: on the one hand, the brave, the witty, the courteous, the promising; and, on the other hand, the youth who knows no law but his own, who cheats, carouses, kills. Middle age is similarly portrayed in its meanness and its greatness, its selfishness and its compassion. And, finally, Old Age, with experiences past and wisdom gained, speaks out with the privilege of the aged. He has learned one truth: that "all degrees of men shall find But vanity, vexation of the mind."[14]

IV *"The Four Seasons"*

Finally, there is the fourth quaternion, "The Four Seasons." Though personified like the rest, the seasons are not really given personalities but are merely described, mostly in a conventional and traditional manner. For example, Winter says:

> *December* is the first, and now the Sun
> To th' Southward tropick, his swift race hath run;
> This month he's hous'd in horned *Capricorn,*
> From thence he 'gins to length the shortned morn,
> Through christendome, with great festivity,
> Now's held a Guest (but blest) Nativity.

In summer, the shepherd lads frolic through the landscape in true arcadian fashion:

> Now go those frolick swaines, the shepheard lad,
> To wash their thick cloath'd flocks, with pipes ful glad.
> In the coole streames they labour with delight,
> Rubbing their dirty coates, till they look white.
> Whose fleece when purely spun, and deeply dy'd,
> With robes thereof, Kings have been dignifi'd.
> . . . .
> Carelesse of worldly wealth, you sit and pipe,
> Whilst they're imbroyl'd in Wars, and troubles ripe;[15]

Autumn with its orange, lemon, pomegranate, and fig is hardly the autumn of New England; it is a conventional concept. Not even a New England winter inspires the poet to an original picture. The apprentice poet in "The Four Seasons" was far away from the author of "Contemplations." But Anne Bradstreet was dissatisfied with her own efforts; she was aware of her lame verse as she closed her "four times four" quaternions with an apology addressed to her father:

> My Subjects bare, my Brains are bad,
> Or better Lines you should have had;
> The first fell in so naturally,
> I could not tell how to passe't by:
> The last, though bad, I could not mend,
> Accept therefore of what is penn'd,
> And all the faults which you shall spy,
> Shall at your feet for pardon cry.[16]

V "The Four Monarchies"

In spite of this recognition of her own poor lines, she had to set about another task she gave herself: the poetic version of some of Raleigh's and others' histories of the world. If it were not almost twice as long as the other "four times four" poems put together, one might regard "The Four Monarchies" as a postscript quaternion.[17] It is a poetical version of history from the Assyrian Monarchy to the Roman (the writing of the last monarchy unfinished).

Just how do these five lengthy poems of rhyming couplets stand up as poetry? To a large extent we shall have to agree with the critics who have said that "On the whole these poems are tedious, unleavened by imaginative power, and cramped by diction. She never mastered the pentameter couplet." "The painstaking elborations of the 'quaternions' interests the modern reader only as survivals of medieval jugglery."

"The Four Seasons" is conventional, imitative, unoriginal; but, as pastoral poetry, it is far better to read than the historical narrative of "The Four Monarchies." As many critics have said, it was fortunate that the final pages of the "Monarchies" went up in flames with the Bradstreet house. The reading of the third and the unfinished fourth monarchy is a chore. We feel instinctively that the author is bogging down under the strain of the gigantic task she has set herself. The portraits in the fourth monarchy are shorter, but that does not make them better. With dogged determination, the poet puts couplets together, telescoping the facts of history, and the result is a monotonous singsong:

> Next, *Servius Tullius* sits upon the Throne,
> Ascends not up, by merits of his owne,
> But by the favour, and the speciall grace
> Of *Tanaquil*, late Queen, obtaines the place;
> He ranks the people, into each degree,
> As wealth had made them of abilitie;
> A generall Muster takes, which by account,
> To eighty thousand soules then did amount:
> Forty foure years did *Servius Tullius* reigne,
> And then by *Tarquin, Priscus* Son, was slaine.[18]

The only virtue of this poem is its brevity.

The reader who has pursued a conscientious chronological reading of the first edition of Anne Bradstreet's poetry may have grown so fatigued by the time he has reached the last page of "The Four Monarchies" that he has lost sight of all possible virtues of the preceding poems, and turns with jaundiced eye to those few remaining. Yet there are in the apprentice author of *The Tenth Muse Lately Sprung Up in America* some indications of the craftsman of the poems of later editions.

In the first place, the book reveals an intelligent and well-educated mind, prerequisites for a writer of any sort. Her reading was varied and superior for anyone of her age, man or woman, who did not pretend to reach the galaxy of stars of the seventeenth century. She had the habit of naming authors whom she had read. They were many and their subject matter varied, but history and science, particularly anatomy, were the subjects of her greatest interest. She knew some authors of the classics. This evidence of her education and reading is contained for the most part in *The Tenth Muse*.

The difficulty with identifying sources for specific passages in her work is that she was very careful to avoid plagiarism.

In the dedication of her first work to her father she assured him, "My goods are true (though poor) I love no stealth." She did paraphrase much of Raleigh's *History*, as parallel passages in the two works show; but she could not have been expected to be creative in dealing with the facts of history, which she had to derive from some source. Other historians she mentions are Camden and Speed (for English history), Curtius, Pemble, Ussher, Plutarch, and Xenophon. Some were not necessarily primary sources. While North's translation of Plutarch was in Puritan libraries and she could easily have read it in English, some others like Ussher's *Annales Veteris* and Camden's *Annales Rerum Anglicarum* . . . were not in translation.

There is no proof that she could read Greek or Latin. Her references to Aristotle, Homer, Plato, and Pliny were commonplace; the Muses, Daphne, Jupiter, Vulcan, and the names of the Zodiac to which she refers were known by all educated Puritans. If her use of Greek and Latin sources had been more specific or more frequent, we could assume either that she knew these languages or that her father or her husband, a graduate of Cambridge, translated for her.

She cites the classical names of Galen and Hippocrates in her enthusiastic excursions into the subject of anatomy and also Crooke, the English doctor. Ellis is inclined to believe she learned most of her facts concerning anatomy from Crooke's *Description of the Body of Man*, a standard text that compiled all the known facts of anatomy, for she mentions the author more than once. If she read Crooke, she did well to glean her facts from a book that tangles science with astrology, a subject that the Puritans rejected. It is to be remembered, too, that Anne Bradstreet must have learned a great deal of medical science from her own invalidism.

But the sources for her historical or anatomical facts are not so intriguing as suggested sources for her more imaginative flights in poetry.[19] Of her debt to Du Bartas for the wretched pattern of her early poetry we need say no more.

Ellis sees "some passages in her 'Poems' which seem as if they must have been suggested by a reading of Shakespeare," a source which she would not have made obvious considering the Puritans' complete rejection of Elizabethan dramatists. But Ellis is overly cautious and inconsistent when he says that "With the plays of Shakespeare, as well as those of Ben Jonson, Beaumont and Fletcher, Middleton, Webster, Massinger, and the other dramatists, we may well presume that she was not familiar, and that she shunned them, as irreligious."[20] The assumption of this critic and others that Anne Bradstreet shunned Shakespeare as irreligious is inconsistent with echoes of the dramatist that sound throughout her work. Moreover, Mistress Bradstreet was not a symbol of Puritan intolerance.

At first it might be supposed that Anne Bradstreet's favorite figure of the world as a stage might have been suggested by her favorite author, Du Bartas, who wrote, as translated by Sylvester, "The World's a Stage, where God's omnipotence,/His Justice, Knowledge, Love, and Providence/ Do act their Parts. . . .[22] Also, in the "Argument" to "the Sixth Day of the First Weeke," of *The Divine Weekes* there occur the words of Sylvester, "Here, on the Stage, our noble Poet brings. . . ." And, further, in a sonnet by G. Gaywood, among introductory poems to the work in honor of Sylvester, is the line "Makes Heav'n his subject, and Earth his stage, the Arts his Actors." The triple occurrence of the figure within a few pages in a book that Anne Bradstreet admired would seem strong evidence that it was her source. It might, in fact, have lent emphasis to her choice. However, further resemblance between her use of the metaphor and these examples ends there. Du Bartas' explanation is biblical and theological; Anne's is not.

At this point, Anne Bradstreet's and Shakespeare's uses of the metaphor take on greater similarity. Both derive their actors from the passing scene. Although Jaques, in *As You Like It,* philosophizes about seven ages of man and Anne

Bradstreet about only four, both describe the parts their ages play upon the stage of life, and we are sure both have seen the people whom their actors represent. (It can be argued that Anne chose four instead of seven either to fit her scheme of quaternions or, since she shunned plagiarism, to avoid a too close resemblance to Shakespeare, particularly since he was unacceptable to most of her Puritan contemporaries.) There are other similarities: Jaques begins, "All the world's a stage," and proceeds with an explanation of the seven acts. Anne begins, "Lo, now four act upon the stage," and proceeds with her description. The most striking similarity occurs toward the end of each poetic discourse when Jaques says, "Last scene of all that ends this strange eventful history," and Anne, "And last of all to act upon this stage." The similarity is too close to be ignored even though the poets' concepts of the last actor are quite different: he sees Old Age as senile in mind and body; she sees that, although he leans upon a staff, he has gained wisdom through the years.

The evidence of Shakespearean influence upon Anne Bradstreet accumulates as we read through the pages of her poetry. Some bucolic scenes in her "Four Seasons" resemble not only those in Shakespeare's *As You Like It* but also the work of Sidney, Lodge, and Fletcher. The shepherds and shepherdesses are like those that cross the pages of many pieces of Elizabethan literature. Yet there is a persistent echo of Shakespeare in such lines as:

> The cleanly huswives Dary, now's ith' prime,
> Her shelves, and Firkins fill'd for winter time.
> The Meads with Cowslip, Hony-suckl's dight,
> One hangs his head, the other stands upright:

And there are some of the idyllic concepts of Shakespeare, Sidney, and others in:

> Now go those frolick swaines, the shepheard lad,
> To wash their thick cloath'd flocks, with pipes ful glad.
> In the coole streames they labour with delight,

Rubbing their dirty coates, till they look white.
Whose fleece when purely spun, and deeply dy'd,
With robes thereof, Kings have been dignifi'd.

The feeling and the spirit of the pastoral setting in these
two quotations is most reminiscent of the characters in Act
IV, scene iii of *The Winter's Tale.* Scene iii is introduced by
Autolycus, who is singing a lyric that mixes the beauty of
nature with domestic accomplishments—daffodils and "The
white sheet bleaching on the hedge." And presently the
Clown enters and ponders what he needs for sheep shearing
and the accompanying feast.

There are many other lines of the Bradstreet poems that
remind one of passages from Shakespeare: "Nor withering
age shall 'ere come there" bears a similarity to "Age cannot
wither her"; and the fate of Calisthenes, who "lov'd his
master more than did the rest, As did appear, in flattering him
the least," to that of Cordelia.

If each of these parallels is considered separately, the
evidence of direct sources is tenuous indeed; but the cumula-
tive effect adds considerable weight to the belief that she
was familiar with Shakespeare's plays. Other evidence is to
be found in the second edition of Anne Bradstreet's work,
discussed below in Chapter 4.

The device of a play on words, so often used by Elizabethan
poets and notably by Shakespeare and Sidney, is cautiously
and infrequently tried by Anne Bradstreet. Youth, as he is
thought to be by others, is: "As *vain* as froth, or *vanity* can
be, That who would see *vain* man, may look on me."[23]* On
page 90 of the first edition is an example of a play on words:
"Which *Law* includes all *Lawes,* though *lawlesse* stil, And
makes it *lawful Law,* if he but wil; . . ." In the second edition
she discarded this, but she inserted on page 92 (the equivalent
of page 88 of the first):

* Words and their derivatives that are repeated are italicized by
the editor.

If ever King equal'd his *happiness.*
(Quote he) that man for *happy* we commend,
Whose *happy* life attains an *happy* end.

Finally, between pages 197 and 203 occur three passages using a play on words. In the first example, her enthusiasm for Du Bartas, whom she is praising, carries her into a quadruple use of her repetitive scheme:

Sure *liberall* Nature, did with *Art* not small,
In all the *Arts* make thee most *liberall*;
A *thousand thousand* times my *senslesse* Sences
Movelesse, stand charm'd by the sweet influences,
More *senselesse* then the Stones to *Amphions* Lute . . .

In the poem "In Honour of Queen Elizabeth," in the second example of this cluster, she uses the device three times. In addition she uses the paradox twice with repetitive words and once without.

Since first the Sun did *run,* his ne'r *runn'd* race
And earth had twice a yeare, a new old face:
Since *time* was *time,* and *man unmanly man,*
Come shew me such a *Phoenix* if you can?

In the third example she uses repetition not only for meaning but for rhythm:

But *happy England,* which had such a Queen,
O *happy, happy,* had those dayes still been,
But *happinesse,* lies in a higher sphere,
Then wonder not, *Eliza* moves not here.
Full fraught with honour, riches, and with dayes:
She *set,* she *set,* like *Titan* in his rayes, . . .

A similar use of "happy" occurred in the lines she substituted in the second edition, "If ever King equal'd his happiness," quoted above. Another example of her use of repetition for emphasis is further enhanced by alliteration.

"From pipe to pot, from pot to words, and blows," which occurs on the same page as the quotation above, "As vain as forth. . . ."

Her use of repetitive devices seems experimental since they occur in clusters within a few pages of her book. Nevertheless, they are as successful as some of those created by Elizabethan and seventeenth-century writers.

If Anne Bradstreet could not openly acknowledge Shakespeare because of the Puritans' quarrel with the English stage, she could acknowledge a classical writer who had considerable impact upon Elizabethan dramatists. Seneca was probably regarded by the Puritans as one of those "virtuous pagans" who could not help the fact that he was not in a state of grace since he had lived before the Christian era; he was probably acceptable because he was also a philosopher.[24] It would be possible to assume that Anne Bradstreet's acquaintance with him was derived from Raleigh's quotation of Seneca's censure in a passage parallel to one in "The Four Monarchies"[25]—possible, if it were not that she embellishes Raleigh's mild account with a true Senecan bloody demise. Calisthenes is put to death by Alexander because the former failed to see his master as a deity:

> He on the wrack, his limbs in peeces rent,
> Thus was he tortur'd, till his life was spent.
> Of this unkingly deed, doth *Seneca*
> This censure passe, and not unwisely, say,
> Of *Alexander,* this th' eternall crime,
> Which shall not be obliterate by time.[26]

Another example of horror is her account of the queen's revenge when she learns of Xerxes' desire for his brother's "chaste and beauteous Dame." Her description of Queen Amestris is much more vivid than Raleigh's:

> She *Harpy*-like, upon the Lady flew:
> Cut off her lilly breasts, her nose, and ears;
> And leaves her thus, besmear'd with blood, and tears.[27]

The works of Shakespeare and Chaucer are listed in the catalogue of books in the libraries of Harvard and Yale universities in the early eighteenth century. Although the date is beyond the time of Anne Bradstreet's life, the books in these libraries were acquired largely as gifts from personal libraries long in the possession of their donors. The listing of these two poets indicates that they were read in the New England colonies. Cotton Mather refers to Chaucer more than once. And Nathaniel Ward, in his praise of Anne Bradstreet, has Apollo say: "And chode buy *Chaucers* Boots, and *Homers* Furrs,/Let men look to 't, least women weare the Spurs."

The evidence that she read Chaucer and was influenced by him is again evanescent but persistent. Her portrait of Youth is Chaucerian, for his face was "as fresh as is Aurora fair." And his character and deeds seem a composite of the best in the squire, the knight, and the clerk. Here is reminiscent image of the young squire conscientiously serving his apprenticeship toward knighthood:

> Of Science, Arts, and Tongues, I know the rules,
> The manners of the Court, I likewise know,
> Nor ignorant what they in Country do;
> The brave attempts of valiant Knights I prize,
> That dare climbe Battlements, rear'd to the skies;
> The snorting Horse, the Trumpet Drum I like,
> The glistring Sword, and wel advanced Pike;
> I cannot lye in trench, before a Town,
> Nor wait til good advice our hopes do crown:
> I scorn the heavy Corslet, Musket-proof,
> I fly to catch the Bulletin that's aloof . . .

"The Four Seasons" also suggest Chaucerian influence: In Spring:

> My second month is *April,* green, and fair,
> Of longer dayes, and a more temperate air;
> The Sun now keeps his posting residence
> In *Taurus* Signe, yet hasteth straight from thence;
>
> . . . .

This is the month whose fruitful showers produces
All Plants, and Flowers, for all delights, and uses.

In Winter:

December is the first, and now the Sun
To th' Southward tropick his swift race hath run;
This month he's hous'd in horned *Capricorn,*
From thence he 'gins to length the shortned morn,
Through *Christendome,* with great festivity
Now's held, a Guest, (but blest) Nativity.

A new season has come, a time for a great religious
"feastivity"[28] throughout Christendom. The resemblance of the
season, pilgrims, and the celebration to the Canterbury
Pilgrims' occasion is, indeed, very remote; yet it somehow
strikes a reminiscent note. What could be more natural than
for the apprentice poet, who imitated without exact copying
and who absorbed all that she read, to pick another season
and another occasion of Christian celebration than those
described by Chaucer?

In the end, what have we found in the five long poems?
Our poet has imitated the verse structure but not the content
of Du Bartas. She has paraphrased in her own way the
History of Sir Walter Raleigh. It would have been unnatural
and unbecoming of her if she had not used biblical references,
which would be easily recognized by her contemporaries and
therefore needed no acknowledgments. There are echoes of
thought and poetic devices of other writers. She had read
much and had absorbed a great deal. The diversity of suggested influences and the cautious, and sometimes clustered,
use of devices and methods—the play on words and the few
trials in Senecan tragedy—suggest experimentation. Actually,
the apprentice was trying out her tools under the guidance of
her masters. The four times four plus one quaternions had
their place in her poetic development. The writing of the
five long poems was a discipline she imposed upon herself

that was remarkable for anyone, particularly someone in chronic ill health and living in a wilderness. This discipline, however dubious its results, prepared the way for her ultimate emancipation from apprentice to craftsman. Even so her "goods were true," as she then felt them to be; and some of the quaternions are worth the reading.

The best indications of the poet to come are in "The Four Humours of Man" and in some of the shorter poems in *The Tenth Muse*. In the portrait of childhood and in others of the four ages of man, we find a warmth and an understanding of character that must have come, not out of the pages of history, but from the poet's own understanding, the substance of all writing that is to endure, the substance that was to be characteristic of her later poetry.

VI *The Elegies*

In the other poems that end the volume, she retains the crippling rhyming couplet, but she is no longer paraphrasing or imitating other authors. She is at last striking out on her own. Even though her first two elegies—to Du Bartas and to Sidney—are in praise of poets she admires and imitates, and even though they are full of conventional references to the other nine muses, her praise in her heroes' honor and her own humility in the presence of their genius are sincere and personal.

The most enthusiastic of the three elegies is on the recent sovereign she most admired, Queen Elizabeth I. As if the great queen had just died, Anne Bradstreet proclaims her worth "In Honour of that High and Mighty Princess Queen Elizabeth of Happy Memory." Although the queen died before her admirer was born, little Anne must have been nurtured on the tales of the great sovereign whom her father had once served in the war against Philip II of Spain. The poem departs from the narrative manner of the quaternions and seems to follow rather loosely the elegiac form. If we may consider the two epitaphs as one or alternate versions, there are the usual three parts: "The Proeme," which pays tribute to one just dead; "The Poem," which recounts her wonderful accomplishments; and "The Epitaph," particularly the second, which rejoices in her undying fame.

The middle part is of exceptional interest, for in it Anne Bradstreet pays tribute not only to Queen Elizabeth as queen but to Queen Elizabeth who glorified the "female sex" and "wip'd off th' aspersion . . . that women wisdome lack to play the Rex." It is a poem in praise of an earthly Minerva. Of great women, this queen is the greatest. She towers above Semiramis, Tomris, Dido, Cleopatra, Zenobya, and is without the infamy of some of these. Anne is obviously biased, and the reader suspects that one of her reasons for writing this poem was to pile up evidence of the greatness of the "female sex." Elizabeth herself is "argument enough to make you mute."

"An Elegie upon that Honourable and renowned Knight *Sir Philip* Sidney, who was untimely slain at the Siege of Zutphen, Anno, 1586" is a poetic, adulatory account of the deeds in "Arms and Arts" of a man who was "no lesse an Honour to our British Land, then she that sway'd the Scepter with her hand." It is full of conventional references to mythological figures: Mars, Minerva, Calliope, Terpsichore were responsible for his genius; his "Rhetorick" struck "Polimina dead"; and his "Eloquence made Mercury wax red"; Euterpe and Clio were "set down." His admirer wished another Homer could "Engrave on Marble, in characters of Gold" the deeds of this modern Achilles. Anne Bradstreet almost completely rewrote this poem for the second edition, displaying her maturing skill as a poet.

The third hero whom she eulogized was, of course, Du Bartas, who "dazzled her sight" and who, alas, made her blind for awhile to the fact that writing poetry is not merely an intellectual exercise. But if this Puritan woman read him, imitated him, praised him, it was no more than did her contemporaries at home and abroad, who enjoyed, as she did, Sylvester's popular translation.

These three elegies, like the other poems, were still chained by rhyming couplets, but they were not mere paraphrases of others' works nor a mere regurgitation of her learning. The poet herself is singing the praise of three great figures whom she admired, two of whom history still recognizes. Certainly Anne Bradstreet was taking a step forward in breaking her chains.

VII *Lamentations*

Of greater poetic worth and the best of the first edition are the two poems that end it: "Of the vanity of all worldly creatures" and "Davids Lamentation for Saul and Jonathan." The latter is a paraphrase of 2 Sam. 1.19, but in spite of this and because of it the poem has beauty of structure and phrasing and achieves some of the musical rhythm and language of David's lamentation:

> Alas, slaine is the Head of *Israel,*
> Illustrious *Saul,* whose beauty did excell,
> Upon thy places, mountan'ous and high,
> How did the mighty fall, and falling dye?
> In *Gath,* let not this thing be spoken on,
> Nor published in streets of *Askelon,*
> Lest Daughters of the *Philistins* rejoyce,
> Lest the uncircumcis'd lift up their voyce:
> O! *Gilbo* Mounts, let never pearled dew,
> Nor fruitfull showres your barren tops bestrew,
> Nor fields of offerings e're on you grow,
> Nor any pleasant thing e're may you show;
> For the mighty ones did soone decay,
> The Shield of *Saul* was vilely cast away;
> There had his dignity so sore a foyle,
> As if his head ne're felt the sacred Oyle.
> Sometimes from crimson blood of gastly staine,
> The bow of *Jonathan* ne're turn'd in vaine,

> Nor from the fat, the spoyles, of mighty men,
> Did *Saul* with bloodlesse Sword turn back agen.
> Pleasant and lovely were they both in life,
> And in their deaths was found no parting strife;
> Swifter then swiftest Eagles, so were they,
> Stronger then Lions, ramping for their prey.
> O *Israels* Dames, o'reflow your beauteous eyes,
> For valiant *Saul,* who on Mount *Gilbo* lyes,
> Who cloathed you in cloath of richest dye,
> And choyse delights, full of variety.
> On your array put ornaments of gold,
> Which made you yet more beauteous to behold.
> O! how in battell did the mighty fall,
> In mid'st of strength not succoured at all:
> O! lovely *Jonathan,* how wert thou slaine,
> In places high, full low thou dost remaine;
> Distrest I am, for thee, deare *Jonathan,*
> Thy love was wonderfull, passing a man;
> Exceeding all the Love that's Feminine,
> So pleasant hast thou been, deare brother mine:
> How are the mighty falne into decay,
> And war-like weapons perished away.

Though she uses the same language and some of the phrasing of the original, Anne Bradstreet achieves a certain new beauty. She also handles the couplets more easily; they are not so frequently closed at the end of the second line either by the idea or by the end of a clause or sentence, even though commas frequently give pause. And, whether she realized it or not, she introduced in many lines an organ note that gave the poem music.

It is appropriate that the first direct record of her spiritual struggle and the last poem of the first edition should be "Of the vanity of all worldly creatures." It is unique in *The Tenth Muse,* for it is the only poem that completely discards imitation and disguised emotions for a forthright, lyric expression of personal thought.

Its place in the volume suggests that when the manuscript of what was to become *The Tenth Muse* left her possession, she was already discarding the pattern of Du Bartas and turning to more original treatment and subject matter. Its actual creation may be pinpointed to January, 1649, between the capture and beheading of Charles I, if one can give an immediate and literal interpretation to the line "He's now a slave that was a Prince of late." In the second edition, she changed this to "He's now a captive that was King of late." A "Prince" could have been used in the more general sense of royalty and for an undetermined time in history—a safer reference at the time of the Puritan revolution; in the revision, it could become more specific, for that political turmoil was over. It is the change from "Prince" to "King" that makes this interpretation more convincing and the date more certain. Moreover, the change and the mood of the poem seem appropriate to the tragic circumstance of 1649: It would seem to mirror the poet's further disillusionment concerning the things of this world. All is in vain, even the status of a king. If this dating is correct, it invalidates Ellis' guess that Woodbridge took the manuscript to England in 1647, or it necessitates the delivery of this poem to the printer by some other means before the publication of *The Tenth Muse* in 1650.

Be that as it may, "Of the vanity of all worldly creatures" is the one poem of the volume that prophesies Anne Bradstreet's independent lyric expression, which—as we have already noted—dominates the work added to the later editions. This characteristic holds true even when one recognizes the influence of a biblical writer. Anne Bradstreet and the author of Ecclesiastes had much in common: both had come to the conclusion that "all's vanity." It holds true, also, even in the light of the tradition of Elizabethan poets whose favorite themes on the serious side were the uncertainty of life and the inevitability of death, as, for example, in the anonymous "On the Vanity of Man's Life,"[29] Thomas Proctor's "Respice Finem" and "A Proper Sonnet, Low Time Consumeth All

Things,"[30] and Chidiock Tichborne's "Elegy."[31] Anne Bradstreet was at home in this tradition:

Of the vanity of all worldly creatures

As he said vanity, so vain say I,
O vanity, O vain all under skie,
Where is the man can say, lo, I have found
On brittle earth, a consolation sound?
What is't in honour, to be set on high?
No, they like beasts, and sonnes of men shall die,
And whilst they live, how oft doth turn their State?
He's now a slave, that was a Prince of late.
What is't in wealth, great treasures for to gain?
No, that's but labour anxious, care and pain.
He heaps up riches, and he heaps up sorrow,
Its his to day, but who's his heire tomorrow?
What then? content in pleasures canst thou find?
More vain then all, that's but to grasp the wind.
The sensuall senses for a time they please,
Mean while the conscience rage, who shall appease?
What is't in beauty? no, that's but a snare,
They'r foul enough to day, that once was fair,
What, Is't in flowring youth, or manly age?
The first is prone to vice, the last to rage.
Where is it then? in wisdome, learning, arts?
Sure if on earth, it must be in those parts;
Yet these, the wisest man of men did find,
But vanity, vexation of the mind,
And he that knows the most doth still bemoan,
He knows not all, that here is to be known,
What is it then? to do as Stoicks tell,
Nor laugh, nor weep, let things go ill or well:
Such stoicks are but stocks, such teaching vain:
While man is man, he shall have ease or pain.
If not in honour, beauty, age, nor treasure,
Nor yet in learning, wisdome, youth nor pleasure?
Where shall I climbe, sound, seek, search or find,
That *summum Bonum* which may stay my mind?
There is a path, no vultures eye hath seen.

Where lions fierce, nor lions whelps hath been,
Which leads unto that living Christall fount,
Who drinks thereof, the world doth naught account.
The depth, and sea, hath said its not in me,
With pearl and gold it shall not valued be:
For *Saphyre, Onix, Topas,* who will change,
Its hid from eyes of men, they count it strange,
Death and destruction, the fame hath heard,
But where, and what it is, from heaven's declar'd,
It brings to honour, which shall not decay,
It steeres with wealth, which time cann't wear away.
It yeeldeth pleasures, farre beyond conceit,
And truly beautifies without deceit.
Nor strength nor wisdome, nor fresh youth shall fade,
Nor death shall see, but are immortall made,
This pearl of price, this tree of life, this spring,
Who is possessed of, shall reign a King.
Nor change of state, nor cares shall ever see,
But wear his Crown unto eternitie,
This satiates the soul, this stayes the mind,
The rest's but vanity, and vain we find.

In summation, the first edition of Anne Bradstreet's poetry, written between 1630 and 1650, when she was between the ages of eighteen and thirty-eight, is the creation of an apprentice working earnestly at her bench, learning to write verse by imitating those whom she admired. There is every evidence that, at the same time, she was using this medium as an outlet for sublimated emotions, the emotions of adjustment in her difficult and often hostile environment and of disappointments and disillusionments as she watched the passing scene.

The poems reveal the alert intelligence of an active mind, one well educated for a female in that day. She was interested in history, medicine, nature, and current events. Though frequently stumbling and tedious, her poetry has its distinctly better moments. We can forget "The Four Monarchies"; we can remember "The Four Humours" as vividly written, perhaps as the covert portrayal of wrangling contemporaries. We can remember "The Four Ages of Man," which must certainly contain the portraits of childhood, youth, middle age, and old age that the author had observed and warmly understood. And we can remember the poems that were less imitative and more original: the *Dialogue* showing her concern for mounting agitation against Charles I; the elegies in honor of two poets and a queen; and finally the two poems that close *The Tenth Muse*.

CHAPTER 4

The Craftsman

K EEPING SECRET the publication of Mistress Anne Bradstreet's poems in 1650 was a kind of triumph on the part of her brother-in-law and other acquaintances. There was connivance among them, for *The Tenth Muse Lately Sprung Up in America* includes versified tributes to her genius by several readers. The publication of the book, with its immodest title, surprised, amused, and shamed its author:

> At thy return my blushing was not small,
> My rambling brat (in print) should mother call,
> I cast thee by as one unfit for light,
> Thy Visage was so irksome in my sight;
> Yet being mine own, at length affection would
> Thy blemishes amend, if so I could. . . .[1]

She saw her "rambling brat" of some two hundred pages of pentameter couplets for what it really was: the creation of an amateur and an apprentice. She set about removing its blemishes, correcting obvious misprints, changing words, adding and substracting lines, improving the rhythm in spots, and sometimes changing the meaning.

Though her script was fairly easy to read, the printer had often bungled the transcription. In her revision, she had to change, for example, "ceases" to "seizes":[2] "So Melancholy seizes on a man." The line with "ceases" does not make sense. She smoothed the original line "Thy love was wonderful, passing a man" (a line that could have been a misprint), to "Thy love was wonderful, surpassing man."[3]

She added lines to make general statements more specific and vivid. The first edition reads: "Upon demand, his mind to *Cyrus* broke,/And told, how Solon in his hight had spoke." She revised this to read:

> The Reason of those words *Cyrus* demands,
> Who *Solon* was? to whom he lifts his hands;
> Then to the King he makes this true report,
> That *Solon* sometimes at his stately Court,
> His Treasures, pleasures, pomp and power did see,
> And viewing all, at all nought mov'd was he:
> That *Cressus* angry, urg'd him to express,
> If ever King equal'd his happiness.
> (Quoth he) that man for happy we commend,
> Whose happy life attains an happy end.[4]

The improvement from an inanimate passage to a lively one is obvious. And, incidentally, there is a moral not expressed in the version of the first edition.

An awkward line, like "More useful then the rest, don't reason erre," was changed to the easier "Of greatest use, if reason do not erre."[5]

On the other hand, she seemed unable to improve very much the lines "Sweet music rapteth my harmonious Soul,/ And elevates my thoughts above the Pole." She changed them to "Sweet music raps my brave harmonious Soul,/My high thoughts elevate beyond the pole."[6] The language is less stilted, however, and this is certainly a forward step in poetic workmanship.

Sometimes a change brought the image into sharper and more immediate focus, as when she changed the original word "world" to "day" in "And then methought the day at noon grew dark." In her revision of this line she also omitted commas about "methought" to make the word no longer parenthetical but direct.[7]

The change of a word sometimes made her meaning more explicit and truer to reality. In the first edition the cock had a "clanging voyce," an image difficult to conceive; but she changed this to read "But waking glad to hear the cocks shrill voice." The original line was also awkward in rhythm: "But do awake, at the cocks clanging voyce."[8]

In her youth Anne Bradstreet had smallpox, and it is Youth who says in the first edition "Sometimes the loathsome Pox, my face be-mars,/With ugly marks of his eternal scars." This clear picture is composed out of experience. For once, we catch a glimpse of the face of the author, and we realize she had another cross to bear. Perhaps, in her revision of these lines, she was thinking not only of the actual phenomenon of inward scars but the psychological: "Sometimes the two fold Pox me sore be:marrs/With outward marks, & inward loathsome scars."[9] Both versions are realistic, and the present tense accompanied by "sometimes" shows that the effect of her illness was still with her, "bemarring" her physically and psychologically, all the days of her life. Is this why there is no portrait of Mistress Anne Bradstreet? Only her brother-in-law, among the poets prefacing or ending the first and second editions, refers to her face; and he might have meant by "native beauty" the beauty that was hers by birth, or her beauty of character, when he wrote: "There needs no painting to that comely face,/That in its native beauty hath such grace."[10] Whatever the significance of her lines, both the first and second versions have their place among the more vividly written parts of her poetry.

It would be impossible here to discuss or list all her revisions of words or phrases for smoother poetic lines. Not a page is without one or more such changes; all are evidence of her dissatisfaction with her first efforts in poetry.

Probably the most interesting revisions are the changes in words, phrases, or lines to suit the contemporary scene. In the revision on Fire, four lines are inserted,

> And stately *London*, (our great *Britain's* glory)
> My raging flame did make a mournful story,
> But maugre all, that I, or foes could do
> That *Phoenix* from her Bed, is risen New.[11]

These lines, of course, place their revision after September, 1666, when the Great Fire of London took place. If, as would be natural, she revised in a chronological page-by-page way, a great part of the revision would have been done sixteen years after the publication of *The Tenth Muse*. The date is also six years after the Restoration of Charles II. She must, therefore, adapt her poetry to the times. This would not be hypocritical. She was a Royalist by early association in the household of the Earl of Lincoln. Moreover, "Old Age" has seen:

> The desolation of a goodly State,
> Plotted and acted so that none can tell,
> Who gave the counsel, but the Prince of hell.

How desolate and how bloody is not told until, in her revision, a savage curse is pronounced by Old Age upon the "hellish miscreants" during the 1641 Insurrection in Ireland:

> Three hundred thousand slaughtered innocents,
> By bloudy Popish, hellish miscreants:
> Oh may you live, and so you will I trust
> To see them swill in blood until they burst.

And then he adds: "I've seen a King by force thrust from his throne,/And an Usurper subt'ly mount thereon."[12]

Has Cromwell become in her eyes a "Usurper" or, considering her distress at the approach of civil war in 1642, did she always think so? At any rate, the point of view in her revision suited the times. When *The Tenth Muse* was published, Charles I had just been beheaded; when she rewrote this section, Charles II was on the throne. But is she able, after all, to say completely and exactly what she thinks? What does she mean by the last two lines spoken by Old Age, which she added for the second edition: "What are my thoughts, this is no time to say. Men may more freely speak another day"? Is it monarchy she fears or is it local Puritan opinion?

But the edition of 1678 did not consist merely of the revised *Tenth Muse*; it also included poems she had been preparing for the second publication: "To the Memory of my dear and ever honoured Father Thomas Dudley Esq.; . . ." (1653); "An Epitaph On my dear and ever honoured Mother Mrs. Dorothy Dudley" (1643); and "Contemplations," "The Flesh and the Spirit," "The Author to Her Book." Added to these were "Several other Poems made by the Author upon Diverse Occasions, . . . found among her Papers after her Death, which she never meant should come to publick view; amongst which, these following (at the desire of some friends that knew her well) are here inserted."[13] These are "Upon a Fit of Sickness" (1632), "Upon Some Distemper of Body," "Before the Birth of one of her Children" (Ellis' title), "To my dear and loving Husband," three letters to her husband, a poem to her father.

For the fourth edition of her work, in 1867, John Harvard Ellis added "Occasional Meditations," in poetry, ranging in dates from 1656-69, and "Meditations Divine and Moral," in prose, dated 1664.

The additions to *The Tenth Muse* will not be discussed here chronologically either as to time of writing or publication date. There is not sufficient marked evidence in change of content or in style to merit it except, perhaps, for those expressing her spiritual struggle which have already been discussed in Chapter 1. There is, however, a common denominator to all of the poems of later editions. Anne Bradstreet was at last identifying herself with her poetry, as only a few poems in *The Tenth Muse* had hinted she might do, these few being the elegies in honor of her heroes and "of the vanity of all worldly creatures." In the later editions, she was identifying herself with her poems in lyric verse instead of in long stretches of rhyming couplets. The subject matter was herself and her family and not ancient heroes of history or personified abstractions. All of these, in contrast to the imitative verse of *The Tenth Muse*, merit the term "original."

I   *Religious Meditations*

The poems of her religious meditations, kept in manuscript till the middle of the nineteenth century, may have been withheld by her descendants because they were too personal to be displayed before the eyes of strangers. Certainly Anne Bradstreet kept them for her children only. Their repeated evidence of physical and spiritual agony has already been discussed in the chapter on her Christian pilgrimage. Their prosody is another matter.

In spite of the fact that these poems were intimately her own, both subject and manner owe some debt to the Bay Psalm Book, published ten years before *The Tenth Muse* and actually the first book published in America. It was written for the Puritan church in America, accepted by it at once, and used constantly in the years after its publication. Anne Bradstreet probably sang from it at every church service she attended after its adoption. Its contents are, of course, the psalms of David, translated literally from the Hebrew and set to already accepted hymn tunes, a task likely to have disastrous results at the hands of even the most expert editors. The Bay Psalm Book, created by Richard Mather *et al.*, was no exception, a fact recognized and excused in its famous preface by Richard Mather, who explained that they intended only a "plain translation," attending "conscience rather than Elegance."[14]

The meditative poems of Anne Bradstreet show strong evidence that they were patterned after the Bay psalms though with much happier results, for she was neither translating nor paraphrasing except for an occasional echo. Their verse form is the same: the ballad stanza of four lines of alternating iambic tetrameter with iambic trimeter or four lines of iambic tetrameter, rhyming *abcb*. In feeling there is one great difference between the psalms and the meditations: in the former, we have the impression of a great leader and of a whole tribe for whom he is praying for deliverance from their enemies; in the latter, the impression of an individual praying for deliverance from her personal distress. Both, however, have apparent intimate contact with their God: they address Him directly and sing hymns of praise when He answers. We may briefly compare their pleas; for instance, in Psalm xxvii the poet cries,

> Hide not thy face from mee, nor off
>   in wrath thy servant cast:
> God of my health, leave, leave not mee.
>   My helper been thou hast.

Anne Bradstreet, in the midst of a fever, pleads: "Hide not thy face from me, I cry'd,/From Burnings keep my soul. . . ."[15]

The theme of her poetic meditations is the same as that of Psalm lxvi, which reads as follows in the tortured Bay Psalm Book version:

> With mouth I cryde to him, and with
>   my tongue extoll'd was hee.
> If in my heart I sin regard
>   The Lord will not heare mee.
> But God that is most mighty hath
>   me heard assuredly;
> Unto the voyce of my prayr he
>   list'ned—attentively.
> Blest be the mighty God, because
>   Neither my prayr hath hee,
> Nor yet his owne benignity,
>   turned away from mee.

We may compare this supplication with the Bradstreet lines:

> I sought him whom my Soul did Love
> With tears I sought him earnestly;
> He bow'd his ear down from Above,
> In vain I did not seek or cry.[16]

And also with—

> Praises to him who hath not left
>   My Soul as destitute;
> Nor turnd his ear away from me,
>   But graunted hath my Suit.[17]

The poem from which this last stanza is taken was written "For the restoration of my dear Husband from a burning Ague, June, 1661." The subject is hardly matter for a biblical psalm, yet it fits neatly into the York tune used to sing Psalm lxvi from which the comparative stanza above is quoted. Similarly, "My thankful heart with glorying Tongue" can be set to the popular York tune. And deliverance "from another fitt" (of sickness) and "In thankful acknowledgment for the letters I received from my husband out of England" will fit neatly into the "Old Hundred." Similar patterns can be cut to almost any of these meditative poems.

Certainly we do not sense in her poems a panorama, with the Israelites being delivered from the hands of their enemies, for Anne was not fighting the problems of a tribe but of herself and her family. The worlds of the two writers may seem far apart, but their pleas to God are not. To pray in the plain style and language of the Bay Psalm Book was an easy matter. In imitation, however, she was creating her own poetry, free of stilted pedestrian narrative. In the words of a later poet, she was discarding the "subtleties of intellect" for the "passion and passionate flow of poetry," even though her intellectual exercises in *The Tenth Muse* were never so sophisticated or witty or technically skillful as those to which Coleridge refers.

References to the Romantic poets are not completely out of order, though Anne Bradstreet died just a century before Wordsworth was born and though she never shared their overwhelming genius. Nevertheless, like them she suffered the conflict of Reality and the Spirit, of herself and the times. She wrote her own odes to dejection in some of her hymns and, in true romantic fashion, she composed her biographical confession. She found her refuge in poetry that expressed her feelings about the common things of life as much as if she had been co-author of the philosophy set down in *The Lyrical Ballads*. And ultimately, like the poets to come, she found solace in nature as a revelation of God.

II *Domestic Poems*

A very real part of Anne Bradstreet's conflict with her times arose from her love of life despite a longing for death during repeated attacks of illness. Her verses on the burning of her house on July 10, 1666, give the reader a sudden insight into her gracious and comfortable household. Her self-rebuke, "far be it that I should repine," reveals that she does repine. Her "sorrowing eyes" see where "oft I sat and long did lye." She stands helpless before the ruin of those things she "loved best." Perhaps her treasured possessions that lay in ashes were her last link with her happy life in the Old World. Gone, too, was the evidence of days when she presided as hostess at a table surrounded by guests; gone were the reminders of that happy wedding day of her son:

> Here stood that Trunk, and there that chest;
> There lay that store I counted best:
> My pleasant things in ashes lye,
> And them behold no more shall I.
> Under thy roof no guest shall sitt,
> Nor at thy Table eat a bitt.
>
> No pleasant tale shall 'ere be told,
> Nor things recounted done of old.
> No Candle 'ere shall shine in Thee,
> Nor bridegroom's voice ere heard shall bee.
> In silence ever shalt thou lye;
> Adieu, Adieu; All's vanity.[18]

Within that home had been reared a family for whom she had the greatest affection and about whom she writes very charmingly in "I had eight birds hatcht in one nest," written

in 1658 when five had flown and three remained. The poem
of forty-seven tetrameter couplets sustains the conceit successfully. It is one of her most ambitious attempts to use a
device so very popular in the seventeenth century. In spite of
her children's maturing, she hovers over her brood reminding
herself and them of her care mid pain and joy and of her
ever-present anxiety concerning their welfare:

> Long did I keep you soft and warm,
> And with my wings kept off all harm,
>
> . . . .
>
> Alas my birds, you wisdome want,
> Of perils you are ignorant,
> Oft times in grass, on trees, in flight,
> Sore accidents on you may light.
> O to your safety have an eye,
> So happy may you live and die:
> Mean while my dayes in tunes Ile spend,
> Till my weak layes with me shall end.
> In shady woods Ile sit and sing,
> And things that past, to mind Ile bring.[19]

Among the lyrics of personal experience are those concerning her husband: her terrible loneliness and anxiety during his absences abroad and her joy at his return sing their
way into hymns of prayer for his safe journey and of thanksgiving for his homecoming. "Upon my dear and loving
husband his goeing into England, Jan. 16, 1661" and "In
thankfull Remembrance for my dear husbands safe Arrival,
Sept. 3, 1662" are two of these hymns. In the first, she also
prays for the successful fruition of the matter that was sending
him to England, a delicate mission to win the favor of
Charles II, the new king, for the Massachusetts Colony:

> Lord, bee thou Pilott to the ship,
>   And send them prosperous gailes;
> In stormes and sicknes, Lord, preserve.
>   Thy Goodnes never failes.

Unto thy work he hath in hand,
Lord, grant Thou good Successe
And favour in their eyes, to whom
He shall make his Addresse.[20]

She thanks her God for the letters she receives from her husband, and she sings His praise when he returns. Similar poems were written concerning her son Samuel's journey to England and his safe arrival home. They have already been shown to be similar in structure and feeling to the hymns of the Bay Psalm Book. For our interest, they reveal the devotion of a Puritan woman for her children and husband, especially the latter.

III *Love Poems*

"To My dear and loving Husband" is one of her best-known lyrics, an unashamed declaration of their passionate devotion. It is familiar to everyone who has studied this early period.

If ever two were one, then surely we.
If ever man were lov'd by wife, then thee;
If ever wife was happy in a man,
Compare with me ye women if you can.
I prize thy love more then whole Mines of gold,
Or all the riches that the East doth hold.
My love is such that Rivers cannot quench,
Nor ought but love from thee, give recompence.
Thy love is such I can no way repay,
The heavens reward thee manifold I pray.
Then while we live, in love lets so persever,
That when we live no more, we may live ever.[21]

Of similar content are "A Letter to her Husband, absent upon Publick employment" (Ellis' title) and two other letters on the same subject. One, "As loving Hind," is of interest for the poet's conscious use of seventeenth-century devices of emblems, puns, plays on words, *et cetera*. Like the poem on her children, it is one of the few in which she goes all out for contemporary mannerisms. Yet, in spite of their artificial figures, both of these poems are effective and charming. The second reads:

> As loving Hind that (Hartless) wants her Deer,
> Scuds through the woods and Fern with harkning ear,
> Perplext, in every bush & nook doth pry,
> Her dearest Deer, might answer ear or eye;
> So doth my anxious soul, which now doth miss,
> A dearer Dear (far dearer Heart) then this.
> Still wait with doubts, & hopes, and failing eye,
> His voice to hear, or person to discry.
> Or as the pensive Dove doth all alone
> (On withered bough) most uncouthly bemoan
> The absence of her Love, and loving Mate,
> Whose loss hath made her so unfortunate:
> Ev'n thus doe I, with many a deep sad groan
> Bewail my turtle true, who now is gone,
> His presence and his safe return, still wooes,
> With thousand dolefull sighs & mournfull Cooes.
> Or as the loving Mullet, that true Fish,
> Her fellow lost, nor joy nor life do wish,
> But lanches on that shore, there for to dye,
> Where she her captive husband doth espy.
> Mine being gone, I lead a joyless life,
> I have a loving phere, yet seem no wife:
> But worst of all, to him can't steer my course,
> I here, he there, alas, both kept by force:
> Return my Dear, my joy, my only Love,
> Unto thy Hinde, thy Mullet and thy Dove,
> Who neither joyes in pasture, house nor streams,
> The substance gone, O me, these are but dreams.
> Together at one Tree, oh let us brouze,
> And like two Turtles roost within one house,
> And like the Mullets in one River glide,
> Let's still remain but one, till death divide.
>
> *Thy loving Love and Dearest Dear,*
> *At home, abroad, and every where.*[22]

The best of her poems to her husband is undated and untitled but was written before the birth of one of her children. In those days, birth and death often went hand in hand, and a woman of Anne Bradstreet's delicate health could not be sure of the outcome of her pregnancies. Her resignation to her possible fate and her words of comfort to her husband are among the most moving lines in all of her poetry because they are an effective poetic expression of a woman of noble character and compassion. Not even her nobility is lessened by a hint of jealousy at the thought of a "step Dame"—at least not to one who has become prejudiced in her favor!

> All things within this fading world hath end,
> Adversity doth still our joyes attend;
> No tyes so strong, no friends so dear and sweet,
> But with deaths parting blow is sure to meet.
> The sentence past is most irrovocable,
> A common thing, yet oh inevitable;
> How soon, my Dear, death may my steps attend,
> How soon't may be thy Lot to lose thy friend,
> We both are ignorant, yet love bids me
> These farewell lines to recommend to thee,
> That when that knot's untyd that made us one,
> I may seem thine, who in effect am none.
> And if I see not half my dayes that's due,
> What nature would, God grant to yours and you;
> The many faults that well you know I have,
> Let be interr'd in my oblivions grave;
> If any worth or virtue were in me,
> Let that live freshly in thy memory
> And when thou feel'st no grief, as I no harms,
> Yet love thy dead, who long lay in thine arms:
> And when thy loss shall be repaid with gains
> Look to my little babes my dear remains.
> And if thou love thy self, or loved'st me
> These O protect from step Dames injury.
> And if chance to thine eyes shall bring this verse,

> With some sad sighs honour my absent Herse;
> And kiss this paper for thy loves dear sake,
> Who with salt tears this last Farewel did take.[23]

Her love poems should take their place proudly among others of her century in England. Their theme, however, is always devoted love, never the unrequited or fickle love of so many contemporary lyrics. She may not have attained the skill of a poet like Donne and certainly she had not his sophisticated experience, but there is much that is alike in her poems to her husband and in such a poem as Donne's "The Ecstasy," especially in her line "that when that knot's unty'd that made us one" and his "that subtle knot which makes us man." In view of the accumulation of evidence that she was influenced by Shakespeare, however, the inspiration for her line may be found in *Antony and Cleopatra,* where Cleopatra applies an asp to her arm, "With thy sharp teeth this knot intrinsicate/Of life at once untie . . ." (v, ii, 306).

The poetic love letters written to her husband may also have found their inspiration in Sonnets LXXXIX to C of *Astrophel and Stella,* in which Astrophel mourns the absence of Stella. For both Anne and Astrophel the days are too long, the silent night is filled with sighs and tears, and the absence of the lover is almost unbearable. For each, Phoebus plays his part as he brings the long day or leaves the long night when he departs. Each feels hemispheres apart. Anne pleads:

> *Phoebus* make haste, the day's too long, be gone,
> The silent night's the fittest time for moan;
> But stay this once, unto my suit give ear,
> And tell my griefs in either Hemisphere:
> (And if the whirling of thy wheels don't drown'd)
> The woful accents of my doleful sound,
> If in thy swift Carrier thou canst make stay,
> I crave this boon, this Errand by the way,
> Commend me to the man more lov'd then life,

Shew him the sorrows of his widdowed wife;
My dumpish thoughts, my groans, my brakish tears
My sobs, my longing hopes, my doubting fears,
And if he love, how can he there abide?[24]

Astrophel moans and sighs and feels the separation of a
hemisphere:

Now that of absence the most irksome night,
With darkest shade doth overcome the daie.
Since *Stellas* eyes that wont give mee my daie,
Leaving my *Hemisphere* o'recast with night,
Each day seemes long, and longs for long staied night:
The night as tedious, wooes th' approch of day:
Toyled with dustie toyles of busie day,
  Languisht with horrors of the silent night,
  Suffering the evils both of daie and night . . .
                (from Sonnet LXXXIX)

Anne Bradstreet's unashamed passion for her adored and
adoring husband resulted in a troubled conscience which
expressed itself in the poem that S. E. Morison called "One
of the best expressions in English literature of the conflict
described by St. Paul in the eighth chapter of his 'Epistle
to the Romans'; a conflict that was evidently part of the personal experience of the poetess." "The Flesh and the Spirit"
must have been the experience of this woman surrounded
by Puritans who were theoretically opposed to the world of
the flesh and the devil. (That they were not opposed in
reality to the acquirement of wives or to the begetting of
children is plain to anyone who will read their histories,
journals, or biographies.) "The Flesh and the Spirit" presents
the views of two sisters in a dialogue that is certainly not a
one-sided argument, even though Spirit has the final and
orthodox say. Certainly Flesh's question, "Can Speculation
satisfy/Notion without Reality?" sounds like the questioning
of the troubled Anne. And her determination to follow the

spiritual path simply adds further evidence of the inner conflict when Spirit says—

> Be still thou unregenerate part,
> Disturb no more my setled heart,
> For I have vow'd, (and so will doe)
> Thee as a foe, still to pursue.
> And combate with thee will and must,
> Untill I see thee laid in th' dust.

And having conquered, Spirit will see the City of Revelation
where, with the other Spirits

> From sickness and infermity,
> For evermore they shall be free,
> Nor withering age shall e're come there,
> But beauty shall be bright and clear.[25]

Anne's feeling of the pure and heavenly light and her diction
in this instance recall Spenser's "An Hymne in Honour of
Beauty":

> And with the brightnesse of her beautie cleare,
> The ravisht harts of gazefull men might reare
> To admiration of that heavenly light,
> From whence proceeds each soule enchaunting might.

The dialogue of the Bradstreet poem is written in tetrameter
couplets and is much more skillfully done than the "Dialogue
between Old England and New." The former is the work
of the mature poet, the latter, of the novice. Some of her
brief, compact lines, pregnant with meaning, remind us of
Emily Dickinson's poetry: "Can Speculation satisfy/Notion
without Reality?" Or the following lines from Flesh's speech:

> Art fancy sick, or turn'd a Sot
> To catch at shadows which are not?
> Come, come, Ile shew unto thy sence,
> Industry hath its recompence.
> What canst desire, but thou maist see
> True substance in variety?

Although the content of this poem is, as Mr. Morison has pointed out, similar to that of St. Paul's "Epistle to the Romans," the probable source for its pattern is medieval debate literature. The evidence is particularly strong since the New England poet shows its influence more than once. "The Owl and the Nightingale" heatedly argue their respective superiority in that piece of medieval literature. The personified abstractions of the elements and "humours" in Anne Bradstreet's earlier poems follow the same conduct in the same kind of debate. The poet has not forgotten the pattern of Middle English debates in versified dialogue in her later work, for "The Flesh and the Spirit" is strongly reminiscent of the didactic poem, "The Debate of the Body and Soul." The older poem begins:

> It chanced, as on a winter's night,
> I drowsing lay, ere dawn of day,
> Methought I saw a wondrous sight—
> Upon a bier a Body lay.[26]

Before the Spirit wanders far from the Body, it stands beside the bier, and the debate on their spiritual conflict begins.

The poet who speaks in "The Flesh and the Spirit" is also a spectator who chances to hear the argument. The older poem is much longer and in the end the "hounds of Hell" come for their victim. Anne Bradstreet is content with the debate alone. It is a credit to her artistry that she finds it enough without obtrusive moralizing. Her treatment of the subject is certainly different from that of the unknown poet, but the theme, the introduction, the method of dialogue are strikingly similar.

IV *Elegiac Poems—Her Family*

Her elegiac poems about her loved ones deserve attention. Though some are still written in pentameter couplets, their matter excuses their manner, and their manner shows a vast improvement over her earlier work. All that we

know of Anne's mother is contained in fourteen lines of her
daughter's epitaph for her:[27] she was a worthy matron, a loving mother, an obedient wife, a friendly neighbor—good to
the poor, kind to servants, instructor to her family. She was
also a woman who attended public meetings and church
faithfully and who, praying often in her closet, prepared
ever for death. It is the portrait of a seventeenth-century
"character," the ideal abstraction of a good woman. We conclude that Anne had great respect for her mother but hardly
the admiration she expressed for her father:

> Who more cause to boast his worth then I?
> Who heard or saw, observ'd or knew him better?
> Or who alive then I, a greater debtor?
> Let malice bite, and envy knaw its fill,
> He was my Father, and Ile praise him still.

She is proudly aware of his part in the founding of the
Massachusetts Bay Colony—a man and governor who was
wise, humble, free of ostentation. Best of all, he was undoubtedly responsible for his beloved daughter's education
among books, and, being a learned man, he taught her many
things. His daughter's epitaph sums up his character:

> Within this Tomb a Patriot lyes
> That was both pious, just and wise,
> To Truth a shield, to right a Wall,
> To Sectaryes a whip and Maul,
> A Magazine of History,
> A Prizer of good Company
> In manners pleasant and severe
> The Good him lov'd the bad did fear,
> And when his time with years was spent
> If some rejoyc'd, more did lament.[28]

Most seventeenth-century tombstone epitaphs amuse us. We
smile at this one; yet it is better than most for, though
written by his biased daughter, it is a truer portrait than we
usually find under these circumstances. Dudley was a

learned man, a true patriot, a sincere but stubborn man (an adjective his daughter would never have used) who championed the cause of right as he saw it even when it earned him enemies as well as friends.

Death was a frequent visitor to the young in colonial days, and it did not skip the Bradstreets. It is a wonder that the fragile Anne lived to record her sorrow at the decease of so many of her own family. Like most of us, she wondered why the good die young, but in this late time of her life she knew she must submit to God's will: "With dreadful awe before him let's be mute,/Such was his will, but why, let's not dispute . . ."[29] She wrote these words in a poem on the death of the fourth child of her son Samuel, when the grandchild was "but a moneth, and one day old." His eldest child, Anne, had died in her fourth year and had inspired one of the best of the poet's memorial poems:

> With troubled heart & trembling hand I write,
> The Heavens have chang'd to sorrow my delight.
> How oft with disappointment have I met,
> When I on fading things my hopes have set?
> Experience might 'fore this have made me wise,
> To value things according to their price:
> Was ever stable joy yet found below?
> Or perfect bliss without mixture of woe.
> I knew she was but as a withering flour,
> That's here to day, perhaps gone in an hour;
> Like as a bubble, or the brittle glass,
> Or like a shadow turning as it was.[30]

The years 1669-70 were terrible ones for Samuel. While he was away from home, his wife Mercy died soon after the premature birth of a child, whom he lost soon after. Of his five children by this wife, only one, Mercy, born in 1667, survived.[31] Samuel was Anne's eldest son and possibly her favorite, and his wife was like her own daughter. In infinite sorrow and compassion, Anne grieves for her son's loss even more than for her own:

And live I still to see Relations gone,
And yet survive to sound this wailing tone;
Ah, woe is me, to write thy Funeral Song,
Who might in reason yet have lived long,
I saw the branches lopt the Tree now fall,
I stood so nigh, it crusht me down withal;
My bruised heart lies sobbing at the Root,
That thou dear Son hath lost both Tree and fruit:
Thou then on Seas sailing to forreign Coast;
Was ignorant what riches thou hadst lost.
But ah too soon those heavy tydings fly,
To strike thee with amazing misery;
Oh how I simpathize with thy sad heart,
And in thy griefs still bear a second part:
I lost a daughter dear, but thou a wife,
Who lov'd thee more (it seem'd) then her own life.
Thou being gone, she longer could not be,
Because her Soul she'd sent along with thee.
One week she only past in pain and woe,
And then her sorrows all at once did go;
A Babe she left before, she soar'd above,
The fifth and last pledg of her dying love,
E're nature would, it hither did arrive,
No wonder it no longer did survive.
So with her Children four, she's now a rest,
All freed from grief (I trust) among the blest;
She one hath left, a joy to thee and me,
The Heavens vouchsafe she may so ever be.
Chear up, (dear Son) thy fainting bleeding heart,
In him alone, that caused all this smart;
What though thy strokes full sad & grievous be,
He knows it is the best for thee and me.[32]

In the excerpts from the three elegiac poems just quoted, the author has used the rhyming couplet; but there is no comparison between the effect of these couplets and those used in her long narratives of history and personified abstractions. Though the rhyme and rhythm are sometimes a little rough, the "faltering lines" are infrequent. And the greatest difference, of course, is that these poems have the true feeling of the lyric poet, the record of sincere emotions.

One other poem in memoriam for Samuel's child, Elizabeth, "who deceased August, 1665, being a year and a half old" is of particular interest for its intricate and delicate verse form: two seven-line stanzas of iambic pentameter rhyming *ababccc* and the *c* rhyme of the first repeated in the last three lines of the second stanza. Both end with an Alexandrine. The form is a variation of the rime royale, used by Phineas Fletcher in "The Purple Island"; but the tying of the two stanzas together by repeated rhyme seems to be a Bradstreet device. And within the first stanza is an effective repetition of an idea in artistic balance, "Eternity" with "Everlasting state," and in both stanzas a three-fold repetition of an initial word in different positions. The verse form is expertly composed, and the effect of the whole is one of lyric delicacy of feeling:

> Farewel dear babe, my hearts too much content,
> Farewel sweet babe, the pleasure of mine eye,
> Farewel fair flower that for a space was lent,
> Then ta'en away unto Eternity.
> Blest babe why should I once bewail thy fate,
> Or sigh the dayes so soon were terminate;
> Sith thou art setled in an Everlasting state.

There are other virtues, too, in this poem. She uses alliteration with taste and skill, and her figure of nature is consistent and apt. The alliteration is superbly done with the musical repetition of "f" in the first three lines and of "s" in the last three; the "s" is then carried into the second stanza. Finally the all-important word "fate," echoing its use in the first stanza, closes the poem:

> By nature Trees do rot when they are grown.
> And Plumbs and Apples throughly ripe do fall,
> And Corn and grass are in their season mown,
> And time brings down what is both strong and tall.

But plants new set to be eradicate,
And buds new blown, to have so short a date,
Is by his hand alone that guides nature and fate.[33]

There is an effective use of contrast and parallelism in the two stanzas. The first mourns the passing of the babe, a fair flower, its days "so soon terminate," but comfort comes from the knowledge that the child is "setled in an Everlasting state," a contrast of thought within the stanza. The second stanza notes the death of trees, "Plumbs" and apples, corn and grass at the hand of nature—even new plants and new-blown buds (like the babe) are "set to be eradicate." But it is "his hand alone that guides nature and fate"—the fate of the bud and the child.

Once again there are tones reminiscent of Shakespeare: "Rough winds do shake the darling buds of May,/And summer's lease hath all too short a date" (Sonnet XVIII). And:

When lofty trees I see barren of leaves,
Which erst from heat did canopy the herd,
And summer's green all girded up in sheaves,
Borne on the bier with white and grisly beard,
Then of thy beauty do I question make,
That than among the wastes of time must go. . . .
(Sonnet XII)

Another possible source of influence on this poem—at least the first stanza—is Milton's "On the Death of a Fair Infant Dying of a Cough." The subject matter is the same, the stanza form in both is rime royal (though with Milton the standard rhyme scheme), the figure of the "fairest flower" that was soon blasted is very similar, and "bewailed his fatal bliss" is comparable to "bewail thy fate":

O fairest flower, no sooner blown but blasted,
Soft silken primrose fading timelessly,
Summer's chief honour, if thou hadst outlasted
Bleak Winter's force that made thy blossom dry;

For he, being amorous on that lovely dye
    That did thy cheek envermeil, thought to kiss,
But killed, alas! and then bewailed his fatal bliss.

This elegy was the first of Anne's poems on the death of
her grandchildren. There can be only a guess why she returned to the rhyming couplet in the other memorial poems.
Perhaps she was too disheartened by repeated deaths to
work at this more difficult form. Perhaps she thought the
rhyming couplet more dignified and appropriate for the
subject of death. Perhap her friends and family, with whom
she shared the reading of her poetry, preferred the conserva-
tive form used in *The Tenth Muse*. Whatever the reason,
she did not try her rime royal in anything but "Contemplations." It is possible she was composing that group of poems
at the same time she was writing her memorial poem to
Elizabeth. The stanza form is the same, and both are steeped
in her awareness of nature. This would be seven years before her death at the age of sixty and could make them both,
as they seem to be, the work of the craftsman of later years.

V *Contemplations*

For many reasons, the real maturing of the poet, both in
content and form, comes in her "Contemplations."[34] The
thirty-three stanzas are not a collection of individual poems,
but each can be read separately with complete satisfaction.
They form an integral whole, as the poet's thoughts, in her
contemplation of nature, flow easily from one stanza into
the next. It is autumn and she is entranced with the "delec-
table view" of nature. Surely its beauty and excellence are
manifestations of the glory of God. Her eye rests on a stately
oak, whose branches seem to touch the sky, and she wonders
how many hundred winters it has seen, but even so its time is
nothing in the presence of eternity. She gazes higher into
the "glistering Sun," the "Soul of this World, this Universes
Eye,—No wonder, some made thee a Deity." The earth, birds,

insects, vegetation are revived by the morning sun, the sun that follows its annual and diurnal course, making day and night and the seasons. Its glory is the gift of the Creator.

The poet, with humble eyes, is moved to magnify her Creator, but in the presence of nature she is only aware of her own "imbecility." She hears the small creatures, the grasshopper and the cricket, sing their hymn of praise, and she, "mute, can warble forth no higher layes." She reflects on ages past and man's history from the time of Adam. Looking back from the present "makes things gone perpetually to last" so that "man's conceit" is more "aged than Methuselah." She retells the story of Adam and "our grandame" and her "bloody Cain new born." Who cannot fancy the terror of Cain as he stands before the "Bar of Judgment"? Who cannot help reflecting on the progeny of Adam clothed in sinful livery? Yet we live "so little while we are alive." We spend our time "in eating, drinking, sleeping, vain delight./So unawares comes on perpetual night." Like the seasons, man grows old and dies, yet, unlike them, he remains in oblivion until the final day.

But should the heavens and earth be praised because they last longer? No, they will die; but man will live to endless immortality. The poet marvels at the river which, joined with other rivulets, inevitably reaches its ocean; and so may man press on to his vast mansion. And the fish, who know not why they visit unknown coasts, know not their own felicity. And "sweet-tongu'd Philomel," who even now chants her melodious strain, feels no sad thoughts nor remembers the past nor fears the future. Passing their youth in summer season, the "feathered crew" escape winter into a better region. Man, unlike these, is never free from care and sorrow. This "sinful creature," this "lump of wretchedness," does not learn from his vexations to hope for divine translation. The mariner who confidently sails a smooth sea may be overtaken by sudden storm. So he that feeds on sweets, who takes this earth as if it were his heaven, finds at last in affliction that on earth there is not honor, wealth, or safety, that only above is security. Time, the fatal wrack of mortal things, draws "oblivions curtains" even "over kings." Only he "whose name is grav'd in white stone" shall last and shine when all records and monuments are gone.

The lesson of the poem is there: "The Heavens declare the glory of God and the firmament showeth his handiwork." Yet man—for the most part careless, selfish, unheeding—lives in false security, and he will at last go down to oblivion unless he has an ear and an eye for divine things, his name engraved on the white stone.[35]

In the letter to her children, Anne Bradstreet had said: "That there is a God my Reason would soon tell me by the wondrous workes that I see, the vast frame of the Heaven and the Earth, the order of all things, night and day, Summer and Winter, Spring and Autumne, the dayly providing for this great houshold upon the Earth, the preserving and directing of All to its proper end."

Meanwhile, like Shakespeare, she is impressed by the unalterable and altering changes that time brings to nature and man. In their separate ways the two poets seek the answer to man's problem as he inevitably faces time's destructive force. She sees triumph only for him whose name is "grav'd in the white stone"; and he, for man's noble character "to brave him" against "Time's scythe." The Shakespeare sonnet reads:

When I do count the clock that tells the time,
   And see the brave day sunk in hideous night;
When I behold the violet past prime,
   And sable curls, all silvered o'er with white;
When lofty trees I see barren of leaves,
   Which erst from heat did canopy the herd,
And summer's green all girded up in sheaves,
   Borne on the bier with white and bristly beard,
Then of thy beauty do I question make,
   That thou among the wastes of time must go,

Since sweets and beauties do themselves forsake
  And die as fast as they see others grow;
    And nothing 'gainst Time's scythe can make defence
    Save breed, to brave him when he takes thee hence.

Anne Bradstreet also sees the "fatal wrack of mortal things":

O Time the fatal wrack of mortal things,
That draws oblivions curtains over kings,
Their sumptuous monuments, men know them not,
Their names without a Record are forgot,
Their parts, their ports, their pomp's all laid in th' dust
Nor wit nor gold, nor buildings scape times rust;
But he whose name is grav'd in the white stone
Shall last and shine when all of these are gone.[36]

Man forgets the inevitability of time and change and fails to make the most of life while he has it.

And though thus short, we shorten many wayes,
Living so little while we are alive;
In eating, drinking, sleeping, vain delight
So unawares comes on perpetual night.[37]

Prompted by quite another circumstance, Wordsworth was to say, more than a century and a quarter later—

The world is too much with us; late and soon
Getting and spending, we lay waste our powers:
Little we see in Nature that is ours . . .

In many ways Anne Bradstreet, as we have already noted, anticipated the Romantic poets—Wordsworth by over a century and Thomson by over seventy-five years. At a time when Dryden was perfecting his rhyming couplet and just before the development of the pseudo-Classicism of the eighteenth century, Anne Bradstreet was discarding her formal couplets for freer forms, and was turning from intellectual exercises in rewriting history to the lyric expression of her own personal experiences.

It was, most of all, her genuine delight in nature that made her akin to the later poets. Though her interest in nature might have been stimulated originally in her "Four Seasons" by the backdrops created by Sidney or Fletcher and though she used a few references to popular classical figures like "Phoebus" and "Philomel," she uses such allusions infrequently; she tends to discard the artificial for the real. That she found nature something to know and love was remarkable, since most of her contemporaries must have remembered that day, fraught with uncertainties and danger, when they had landed on the shores of Massachusetts Bay and had begun their fight to push back the forests, the dwelling place of Indians and wild beasts. Anne was different. In Stanza 26 of "Contemplations," she takes sheer delight in nature:

> While musing thus with contemplation fed,
> And thousand fancies buzzing in my brain,
> The sweet-tongu'd Philomel percht ore my head,
> And chanted forth a most melodious strain
> Which rapt me so with wonder and delight,
> I judg'd my hearing better than my sight,
> And wisht me wings with her a while to take my flight.

She finds in nature her own philosophy (Stanza 21):

> Under the cooling shadow of a stately Elm
> Close sate I by a goodly Rivers side,
> Where gliding streams the Rocks did overwhelm;
> A lonely place, with pleasures dignifi'd.
> I once that lov'd the shady woods so well,
> Now thought the rivers did the trees excel,
> And if the sun would ever shine, there would I dwell.

And she sees a comparison and a difference between nature and man (Stanza 18). Nature is her solace, for in it she sees a symbol of everlasting life in a world in which man's days are numbered:

When I behold the heavens as in their prime,
And then the earth (though old) stil clad in green,
The stones and trees, insensible of time,
Nor age nor wrinkle on their front are seen;
If winter come, and greeness then do fade,
A Spring returns, and they more youthfull made;
But Man grows old, lies down, remains where once he's
    laid.

If the chronology had been reversed, critics might have written studies on the influence of the Romantic poets on Anne Bradstreet! Did they read her? Certainly in "Contemplations" one is constantly reminded of some evanescent thought or phrase of the Romanticists: Might not Emerson have said, "the Universes Eye";[38] or Wordsworth, "Living so little while we are alive";[39] or Shelley, "If winter come . . . a Spring returns";[40] or Coleridge, "Where gliding streams the Rocks did overwhelm; A lonely place, with pleasures dignified,"[41] or a half-dozen other sympathetic overtones? These great ones could have read her—apparently many people did,—but the evidence is not sufficiently obvious for positive conclusions. The important thing is that Anne Bradstreet, Puritan poet, felt and wrote as they did about nature and about themselves. Like Cotton Mather in his *Christian Philosopher*, she anticipated not only the Romanticists but the Transcendentalists and their feeling of God in nature.

CHAPTER *5*

The Prose Writer

IT IS APPARENT that Anne Bradstreet, in middle life, experimented in freer and more difficult forms of verse than the couplets of *The Tenth Muse*. During the same period she was trying her hand at writing a prose form that was currently popular: the short epigrammatic or aphoristic essay made famous by Francis Bacon and others and by the writers of "characters," though the "character" portraits had little direct influence on her work except for her elegy on her mother. There were other forces that had an impact upon her prose: the meditation, which had a long history of pietistic writing; the Bible, particularly Ecclesiastes, Psalms, and Proverbs; and emblematic literature, like that of Quarles,[1] if we strip the true "emblem" of its usual accompanying engraving and consider only the moral illustrated by the word picture.

"Youth is the time of getting, middle age of improving, and old age of spending" in Meditation III of her prose writings is a sentence worthy of Bacon. "There is no new thing under the sun" (Meditation XXIV), "he then makes them lye down in green pastures, and leads them besides the still waters" (XX), and " a good name is a precious oyntment" (LXXIII) are obviously of biblical origin; and she specifically names and quotes David, Solomon, and Ecclesiastes. Her use of the Bible throughout her work is of course too extensive to be cited in its entirety.

And, finally, "a shadow in the parching sun, a shelter in the blistering storm" with its accompanying moral is the stuff of which emblems are made. The figures of the "bee" or "wax" or "hive" or "sweetness," which she and others of her generation used, are echoes of emblematic literature. And, in beginning Meditation XL, she says, "spring is a lively *emblem* of the resurrection"; and she continues with other emblematic figures of winter and spring: "leafless trees" and "dry stocks" of temporary death before the Resurrection.

All of these types of writing, which had their influence upon her, had two things in common: they were all short, self-contained pieces written to present a moral, and they were written in an epigrammatic style. The authentic emblem was, of course, a very short didactic poem accompanied by a picture, the figurative emblem of the poetic thought. Stripped of its usual engraving, it was nothing more than a short poetic sermon. Both the emblem and the aphoristic essay were composed not only for the author's pleasure but for a larger audience that might benefit from or at least cogitate upon the moral truths they contained. The meditation was sometimes written for the author himself, but not always. It is doubtful that Cotton Mather, for instance, intended to keep his meditations upon a fireplace to himself.

It was not exactly on impulse or for mere personal gratification that Anne Bradstreet composed her "Meditations." In a letter to her son Simon accompanying this work, she said: "you once desired me to leave something for you in writing that you might look upon when you should see me no more. I could think of nothing more fit for you, nor of more ease to my self, then these short meditations." This preface to him—and, by inference, to all her children—is dated March 20, 1664. The manuscript is entitled "Meditations Divine and morall."[2] She declares that in writing them she has not "encroached upon other conceptions" because she would leave her children "nothing but myne owne."

Despite the influences to which we have alluded, her statement is true. Although her meditations are wholly imitative in manner, they are, except for a phrase here and there, rarely imitative in subject matter. They are the work of a gifted woman who had lived through the hardships of Puritan life in America and through her own personal rebellion to reconciliation and the wisdom of mature years. The two bold words "divine" and "morall" she does not now regard with either skepticism or distaste. The ways of God, however inscrutable, she has accepted—and life too, as she has seen it. Now, with the privilege of years, she dares moralize upon these things so that her children will not, as most do, follow the failings of their parents[3] but will learn the lessons that she has to give them and will follow in the paths of virtue.

The medium which she chose to express these truths was the characteristic didactic paragraph containing epigrammatic sentences in balanced and parallel construction and using figures of speech drawn from life. The love of turning a neat sentence or of composing a poetic conceit among seventeenth-century writers was carried to extremes so that the milder terms of "baroque" prose and "metaphysical" poetry became synonymous with "fantastic" writing. Anne Bradstreet never attained this dubious distinction, for with few exceptions her thought and her style were without self-conscious mannerisms or tortured conceits. These did not interest her, for her chief purpose was to give her children something to remember her by and to think upon.

However, she does use the epigrammatic sentence and the parallel structure, and she does present her lesson through analogies and metaphors drawn from life, but she weaves the whole into one compactly written unit. For instance, Meditation IV reads: "A ship that beares much saile, and little or no ballast, is easily overset; and that man, whose head hath great abilities, and his heart little or no grace, is in danger of foundering."

The amateur writer of parallel structure can founder into monotony by making the parallelism too exact. If he is skillful, however, he will achieve a certain rhythm and more effective comparative thought by varying the length of structure or introducing additional phrases. Meditation IV illustrates a skillful use of variation, for there is a great difference between this and what its author might have written: "A ship that beares much saile but no ballast is easily overset; and a man, who hath great abilities, but no heart is easily foundered." Though the latter is effective and there are classic uses of it in the epigram and in proverbs, it becomes singsong and deadly to the reader when used in a longer essay or in a series of essays such as the meditations. It will be noted, too, that she carries out a consistent figure in this meditation.

She gives another variation to exact parallelism by introducing three parts rather than two: "The finest bread hath the least bran; the purest hony the least wax; and the sincerest christian the least self love" (VI). Variation is achieved here not only by an odd number of parallels but by omitting the repetition of the verb in the second and third parts and by introducing the article in the third.

Meditation XII is an example of a neat, compactly put epigram in parallel structure and consistent figure: "Authority without wisedome is like a heavy axe without an edg, fitter to bruise then polish." This example also illustrates the figure of speech derived from familiar things of everyday life. There are many others in these meditations, too numerous to list completely:

Downy beds make drosey persons, but hard lodging keeps the eyes open (VIII).

. . . .

That house which is not often swept makes the cleanly inhabitant soone loath it, and that heart which is not continually purifieing it self . . . (XVI).

. . . .

Corne, till it have past through the Mill and been ground
to powder, is not fit for bread. God so deales with his
servants, he grindes them with greif and pain till they
turn to dust, and then are they fit manchet for his
Mansion (XIX).

. . . .

The skillful fisher hath his severall baits for severall fish,
but there is a hooke under all; Satan, that great Angler . . .
(XXIII).

Some of her figures are from her own knowledge of illness
and medicine: "sore finger" (XXVI); "concoction," meaning
digestion (XLIV).

One of the interesting things about the Bradstreet meditations is that we can see an almost day-to-day development
in her experiment with this form of writing, assuming, of
course, that they are presented in the order in which they
were written. At first she follows the concise and simple
structure of the short paragraph, as in the examples quoted
above. Compared to those that follow, it is as if she were
taking a trial flight at first in this form of writing; as she
progresses, she discards the model of the proverb and ex-
pands her idea into short essays, like Meditation LXII:

> As man is called the little world, so his heart may be
> cal'd the little Commonwealth: his more fixed and re-
> solved thoughts are like to inhabitants, his slight and
> flitting thoughts are like passengers that travell to and
> fro continually; here is also the great Court of justice
> erected, which is always kept by conscience who is both
> accuser, excuser, witnes, and Judg, whom no bribes
> can pervert, nor flattery cause to favour, but as he finds
> evidence, so he absolves or condemnes: yea, so Absolute
> is this Court of Judicature, that there is no appeale from
> it,—no, not to the Court of heaven itself,—for if our con-
> science condemn us, he, also, who is greater then our
> conscience, will do it much more; but he that would have

boldness to go to the throne of grace to be accepted there, must be sure to carry a certificate from the Court of conscience, that he stands right there.

Meditation LXI comes the nearest of all to placing its author in the "fantastic" school:

> Corne is produced with much labour (as the husband-man well knowes), and some land askes much more paines then some other doth to be brought into tilth, yet all must be ploughed and harrowed; some children (like soure land) are so tough and morose a disposition, that the plough of correction must make long furrows on their back, and the Harrow of discipline goe often over them, before they bee fit soile, to sow the seed of morality, much lesse of grace in them. But when by prudent nurture they are brought into a fit capacity, let the seed of good instruction and exhortation be sown in the spring of their youth, and a plentifull crop may be expected in the harvest of their yeares.

Also, the much shorter Meditation XXVIII uses a play on words: "Wisdome with an inheritance is good, but wisdome without an inheritance, is better, then an inheritance without wisedome."

There is a great difference in the construction of these two meditations. The first is rather involved, but it maintains the usual balance of ideas between the didactic thought and its figurative analogy. The second is written in the pattern she established in the beginning of the series. It is after the thirty-seventh meditation that she adopts a change of pace: she develops her ideas into full-blown essay paragraphs, though there are a few interspersed short aphorisms as if she wished to give variety of length for a more artistic result.

The themes of her meditations are varied, but all are within her experiences and observations through life and books. The subject matter on the whole, however, can be summed up as concerned with Christian living, though a few deal with the petty concerns and duties of daily problems. Meditation X, for instance, must have been inspired by her disciplining of her "diverse" children. "Diverse children have their different natures; some are like flesh which nothing but salt will keep from putrefaction; some again like tender fruits that are best preserved with sugar: those parents are wise that can fit their nurture according to their Nature." Meditation XXV must have gotten its truth and its realistic figure from the author's battle with ill health: "An akeing head requires a soft pillow; and a drooping heart a strong support."

There is a cluster of meditations between XXVI and XXXV that have personal and political overtones of criticism—of political ambitions and short-sightedness. They resemble the veiled criticisms in *The Tenth Muse*.

A sore finger may disquiet the whole body, but an ulcer within destroys it: so an enemy without may disturb a Commonwealth, but dissensions within over throw it (XXVI).

Dimne eyes are the concomitants of old age; and short sightednes, in those that are eyes of a Republique, foretels a declineing State (XXXIV).

Yellow leaves argue want of sap, and gray haires want of moisture; so dry and saplesse performances are simptoms of little spiritall vigor (XXX).

Meditations XLVIII to the last one, LXXVII, are mostly the longer paragraph essays, and their subject is more specifically the relation of God to man and the duties of the true Christian. The author was nearing the end of her life, and it was as if, realizing this, she had much to say about the vanity of this world and the ultimate judgment of God. Her son Simon added this note at the end of the manuscript: "My honored and dear mother intended to have filled up this Book with the like observations but was prevented by Death."[4]

The skillful handling of prose, like the flowering of her poetic gift, came comparatively late to Anne Bradstreet. It is regrettable that there could not have been more years in which to fill up her book with more lyric poetry and experiments in prose.

CHAPTER 6

Epilogue

IT WOULD BE interesting to know what Governor Winthrop, had he lived a year longer, might have said of
the "tenth muse" who had lately sprung up in America. On
April 13, 1645, five years before the publication of her book,
he had recorded in his *Journal* that:

> Mr. Hopkins, the governor of Hartford upon Connecti-
> cut, came to Boston, and brought his wife with him, (a
> godly young woman, and of special parts,) who was
> fallen into a sad infirmity, the loss of her understanding
> and reason, which had been growing upon her divers
> years, by occasion of her giving herself wholly to reading
> and writing, and had written many books. Her husband,
> being very loving and tender of her, was loath to grieve
> her; but he saw his error, when it was too late. For if
> she had attended her household affairs, and such things
> as belong to women, and not gone out of her way and
> calling to meddle in such things as are proper for men,
> whose minds are stronger, etc., she had kept her wits,
> and might have improved them usefully and honorably
> in the place God had set her.[1]

It is to be assumed from this and other evidence that
Winthrop's was the usual attitude toward women in the
Puritan colony and elsewhere. Anne Bradstreet's awareness
of male condescension is reflected in the lines of the Prologue
to her poems:

> Men have precedency and still excell,
> It is but vain unjustly to wage warre;
> Men can do best, and women know it well
> Preheminence in all and each is yours . . .

This, of course, was said with tongue in check. She knew very well that she had taken particular pains to show the superior capabilities of Queen Elizabeth and that she had frequently reminded her readers of the gifts of the nine feminine muses: after all, they had had a lot to do with Sidney's genius. The lines were an ironic gesture of diplomacy, and their "acknowledgment" of man's superiority made it easier perhaps for masculine members of her social circle to forget their prejudices. In any case, the extravagant praise of Anne Bradstreet's contemporaries was certainly extraordinary. But then Anne Bradstreet was an extraordinary woman who performed the social duties of an executive's wife and "attended her household affairs, and such things as belong to women," yet gave a good part of her time to reading and writing—and kept her wits besides.

The laudatory verses of those who were let in on the secret of the publication introduce the poems of *The Tenth Muse*. Nathaniel Ward, whose name is almost synonymous with orthodoxy and intolerance, but whose language is quaintly unorthodox, called her "a right Du Bartas Girle"—or, if we believe him, it was Mercury and Minerva who said it when they presented Apollo (who seems to have lost his youthful charm) with books by Du Bartas and Bradstreet and asked him which was better. Apollo, using "the best brains he had in's old pudding-pan," could not find the answer, but it did revive his "frost bitten blood, To see a Woman, once, do ought that's good."[2]

John Woodbridge, who was responsible for smuggling the manuscript to England, is, of course, equally admiring. At the same time, he is careful to explain that Anne was not like other women: "If women, I with other women may compare,/

Your works are solid, others weak as Air." And he insists "That for a woman's Work 'tis very rare."[3]

Other poems of praise are variously signed "C. B.," "N. H.," "H. S." One printed in the first edition, but omitted in the second, is written in pretended terror at this manifestation of the rise of women in the world.

Arme, arme, Soldado's arme, Horse,
Horse, speed your Horses,
Gentle-women, make head, they vent their plots in Verses;
They write of Monarchies, a most seditious word,
It signifies Oppression, Tyranny, and Sword:
March amain to *London*, they'l rise, for there they flock,
But stay a while, they seldome rise till ten a clock.

R.Q.[4]

There were seven complimentary verses introducing the first edition of Mistress Bradstreet's poems. Obviously the poems' first reading was not contained within the bosom of her immediate family, and village gossip must have spread the news that the governor's daughter was scribbling verse. At any rate, there were some whose tongues wagged in disapproval of "female poets." She speaks of "carping tongues" in the Prologue to the first edition of the poems, referring either to disapproval already expressed before publication or to that anticipated. She is

. . . obnoxious to each carping tongue
Who says my hand a needle better fits,
A Poets pen all scorn I should thus wrong,
For such despite they cast on Female wits:
If what I do prove well, it won't advance,
They'l say it's stoln, or else it was by chance.[5]

This passage reminds one of Du Bartas' "Hence prying Critickes, carping past your skill."[6]

There are at least two British references to Mrs. Bradstreet's poetry. Edward Phillips, nephew of Milton, in his

"Women among the Moderns Eminent for Poetry" in *Theatrum Poetarum* (1675), gave her brief but complimentary notice: "Anne Bradstreet, a New England Poetess, no less in title, viz. before her Poems, printed in Old England anno 1650; then the Tenth Muse Sprung up in America, the memory of which Poems, consisting chiefly of Descriptions of the Four Elements, the four Humours, the four Ages, the four Seasons, and the four Monarchies, is not yet wholly extinct."

Elizabeth Wade White, citing this familiar quotation from Phillips, also discovered a more remote source of reference in *An Essay to Revive the Ancient Education of Gentlewomen in Religion, Manners, Arts & Tongues,* published in London in 1673. Its author, Mrs. Bathsua Makin, after defending the writing of poetry by women of "natural endowments," clarifies the part they must take in "Universal improvement in all kinds of learning. A good Poet must know things Divine, things Natural, things Moral, things Historical, and things Artificial; together with the several terms belonging to all Faculties, to which they must allude. Good Poets must be universal Scholars, able to use a pleasing Phrase, and to express themselves with moving Eloquence."[7] Specifically she says, "How excellent a Poet Mrs. Bradstreet is (now in America) her works do testifie."

Miss White makes the significant point that Phillips' and Makin's praise in 1673 and 1675, respectively, came over twenty years after the publication of *The Tenth Muse,* a tribute to the fact that her poetry was certainly "not wholly extinct." This praise is all the more remarkable since her best poetry had not yet been published.

The English poet "now in America" had met the requirements of a good poet as set down by Mrs. Makin. There was nothing new about them; they were, rather, the ideal of seventeenth-century learning, epitomized in Francis Bacon's desire to take all learning to be his province. While few achieved his success in this endeavor, the man of learning was symbolic of Bacon's period and of the years of the seventeenth century following his death; but the woman of learning was another matter. Our "female" poet in America displayed, for her age and her sex, a remarkable knowledge of books—not always profound but certainly broad and cultivated. In *The Tenth Muse* are "Things Divine, Things Natural, Things Moral, Things Historical, and Things Artificial" together with allusions that display her learning. She was for her time, her place, and her sex as universal a scholar as opportunities and circumstances allowed. Even in her earlier poetry, and certainly in her later, she was clearly able "to use a pleasing Phrase, and to express herself with moving eloquence."

The recognition of Anne Bradstreet's poetry has persisted, though modestly, down through the years. The second edition, revised from the first, appeared in 1678; a third, actually a reprinting of the second, in 1758; the scholarly edition of John Harvard Ellis in 1867; an edition edited by Charles Eliot Norton, one of her descendants, in 1897; and two reprints of the Ellis edition by Peter Smith in 1932 and 1962.

An acceptance of her as a historical phenomenon or a condescending acknowledgment of a degree of poetic worth in her "Contemplations" is as far as some criticism of her work has gone. Charles Eliot Norton, with kindly deprecation, corrected her grammar and spelling in his edition of her work. In his introduction he opined that "in all her poetry" there was "no grace and charm of spontaneous lyrical utterance." F. L. Pattee admits she was "not devoid of poetic feeling" and that "one cannot dismiss utterly a poet who won completely her own generation even when one finds in that poet's work hardly a single element of what modern times demand in its poetry. Like her age, she was fundamentally didactic and always religious."[8]

Max Savelle in his *Seeds of Liberty* (1948) says "Anne Bradstreet's poems, while they do not always treat of religious themes, almost invariably place the feelings in a religious—a

[114]

Puritan setting." This comment is fundamentally different from the preceding one. The first implies a constant imposition of religion and didacticism upon the reader; the second implies a religious *feeling* and a Puritan setting. He who runs may read that Anne Bradstreet was deeply religious, but he should linger awhile to discover that she does not impose either didacticism or religion upon her reader. Her life and her work are framed by a Puritan setting; it would be historically inaccurate to state otherwise. It is equally true that her religion was a deeply personal one and that—contrary to the pious moralizing of which she has sometimes stood accused—she showed admirable restraint.

Moreover, she did not spell out sermons like those of her models Du Bartas and Raleigh, probably because she found the pious utterances of her contemporaries distasteful. In her later poetry, her prayerful hymns were for her own, not another's benefit. And when she wrote the moral and religious—yes, even the didactic piece—"The Flesh and the Spirit," she did not conclude it with a moral tag. To do so would have offended her own taste and ruined the poem's artistry. Never once, in all of her poetry, does she turn directly to the reader and preach a sermon. If a lesson is there, he can read it for himself. It is only in the prose "Meditations," written at the request of her son, that she becomes completely and directly didactic. The occasion called for it, and the meditative form suited her purpose.

Increasing interest in this Puritan woman and her writing has been apparent among American critics of the twentieth century. While they dislike her early efforts—"The Four Monarchies" and in most instances her other quaternions—they praise such poems as her "Contemplations." All recognize the remarkable fact that she wrote at a time that would seem least inspirational to poetic composition, for the business of living and of establishing their religious colony was an all-consuming task for most Puritans. Furthermore, Mistress Bradstreet herself, often in ill health, was busy with the duties of an administrator's wife and of a mother with a large family. Her writing was, of course, a happy and fortunate outlet for pent-up emotions created by her environment. Religious faith and confidence in their cause were the primary factors that sustained most Puritans in their holy adventure in an uncivilized land. At times Anne Bradstreet questioned both. Less courageous women died, like Lady Arbella and Dorothy Bradford, and others may have "gone mad at twenty-one"; but the Puritan woman of this study met the challenge of making a cherished place in her home for her large family and of recording her thoughts and emotions in poetry so that her children would know "what was" their "living mother's mind."

The time has come at last, however, when we have ceased thinking of her only as a remarkable phenomenon, a kind of abstraction of a frail Puritan woman who wrote poetry while setting up several residences and rearing a family in a wilderness. Of course, the fact of anyone's writing against such adverse circumstances is remarkable.

We recognize the publication of *The Tenth Muse* in 1650 as historically important, for it is the first volume of poetry, the first work of *belles lettres*, to come out of America. Indeed, as Miss White[9] and Mr. Pearson[10] point out, she was the first English poetess to have her volume of verse (antedating Katharine Philips' work by a year) outlive other earlier publications by women. "Certainly," says Miss White, "no Englishwoman writing before Anne Bradstreet created a body of verse which has been remembered with so much respect. . . ."

The fact that Anne Bradstreet's poetry was a remarkable phenomenon and historically significant neither makes nor excuses it as poetry. The question is: Did she, in addition, have "the poetic endowment"? Her critics have increasingly perceived that there is much more than historical importance to her work, that it is the creation of a genuine poet.

In 1878, in his *History of American Literature* ("During the

Colonial Time"), Moses Coit Tyler became the first after
John Harvard Ellis (in the able introduction to his edition
of 1867) to give her a really critical appraisal, devoting sixteen pages to his appreciation. He recognized the faults as
well as the virtues of the Bradstreet poems and the un-
sympathetic background against which they were composed:

> In her own writings, as in the writings of her contem-
> poraries, one hears, between the lines, the plaintive cry
> of their consciousness of being, for a sacred duty and by
> God's unmistakable will, in a remote exile:
>
> > 'Remember, Lord, thy folk, whom Thou
> > To wilderness has brought.'

He observes that during the composition of the poems in the
first edition "she had neither leisure, nor elegant surround-
ings, nor freedom from anxious thoughts, nor even abounding
health."[11] Taking note of her "sadly misguided" poetic stand-
ards, he sees, nevertheless, "amid all this lamentable rubbish,
there is often to be found such an ingot of genuine poetry, as
proves her to have had, indeed, the poetic endowment."[12]
The "lamentable rubbish" of which he speaks is, of course,
imitative poetry "of metrical theology and chronology and
politics and physics" in *The Tenth Muse;* the "genuine poetry"
such work as "Contemplations."

In the twentieth century, Conrad Aiken was first after
Tyler to think of the Bradstreet poetry as a genuine part of
our heritage when he used the best of her work in his
anthology of American literature in 1929. In 1938, the Oxford
Anthology, compiled by William Rose Benét and Norman
Holmes Pearson, included several of the poems and meditations. They have been indispensable to anthologies of American literature ever since.

George Frisbie Whicher expressed an admirable, just, and
complete estimate of her poetry in "Alas, All's Vanity, or A
Leaf from the First American edition of Several Poems by
Anne Bradstreet. . . ."

. . . The production of a volume of secular verse, the earliest indubitable piece of *belles lettres* printed in the English colonies, is an event of luminous import. It shows that in the Massachusetts Bay of 1678,* when the strain and turmoil of King Philip's War had barely subsided, there were persons who desired to bring into being such a book as a tangible object to be sold across counters, carried home to meagrely filled shelves, and cherished in the hands of readers.[13]

That estimate was for her own time and history. What is the value of Anne Bradstreet for the twentieth century? Whicher continues:

Her domestic and personal lyrics . . . reach a level of achievement not surpassed by any woman poet for at least a century and may still be included in any anthology purely on their merits. Certainly no representative collection of American poems could afford to omit the disarming and witty lines entitled "The Author to her Book," or the fervent "To My Dear and Loving Husband," or the stanzas on the burning of her house . . . or the devotional lyric . . . "A weary pilgrim. . . ." To these might be added the longer "Contemplations," not because it contains lines that anticipate a famous passage by Shelley, but because it exhibits, along with the conventional poetic apparatus of Phoebus and Philomel, fresh observation of American autumn scenery, pathless woods, and dashing rivers; and "The Flesh and the Spirit" because of its deeply felt restatement of the interior drama of man's destiny, as Puritan theology interpreted it. These six poems . . . stand securely among the first genuinely successful poems written by anyone in this country. . . .[14]

Her highest commendation came from a distinguished scholar of American literature, Samuel Eliot Morison, who said she was the "greatest American poetess before Emily

* The date of the second edition.

Dickinson." The fact of this historical placement is not so important as the sympathetic coupling of the two women poets. Both poured out their thoughts and emotions about their somewhat recluded worlds which, in their respective ways, were sometimes hostile to them. Both wrote without thought of public audience. Their styles and methods were, of course, quite different. At least in the beginning, Anne's poetry was weighted down with learning and with laborious versification; Emily's was ever cryptic and sparing in language. Yet there were times when Anne expressed herself in brief compact phrases worthy of the later poet. Both wrote poetry for its own sake, a fact remarkable for the earlier poet, for the time was not ripe for poetry by men or women.

Another critic of American life and literature, Percy Boynton, while dismissing her quaternions as "survivals of medieval jugglery," wrote an appraisal of her later verse in which he found a sympathetic relationship with other later poets including another distinguished woman poet. "Her 'Contemplations,' " he said, "is as poetic in thought as Bryant's 'Thanatopsis' or Lanier's 'The Marshes of Glynn' or Millay's 'Renascence,' with which it stands in suggestive contrast in the pageant of the ages; and it was far nearer to the spirit of Bryant than Bryant was to the spirit of the latter two. Like Bryant, she dwelt instinctively on the idea that nature endures but man is mortal. It was never long absent from the Puritan mind; though when it came to the average Puritan, it was likely to find no fitter form that in the epitaph."[15]

Anne Bradstreet's verse is, at its best, the work of a woman of real "poetic endowment." Even in her first attempts there are prophecies of better things to come. The earlier poems are the trial flights of the imitative apprentice, yet one with a mind of her own who found in them an outlet for her frustrations and spiritual skepticism in a hostile world. As maturity came, so did spiritual reconciliation and poetic growth. The seventeenth century was a great period of

English writers of poetry and prose, and comparisons are invidious. Yet there are few poets of the seventeenth century not of the highest stature who excel her in true poetic feeling and expression. Whicher's list of her poems that "stand purely on their merits" is a perceptive one. There should be added her elegies, especially the one on Elizabeth, and her letters to her husband, particularly the one written before the birth of one of her children. We would have to look far and long to find a better expression of love and pathos. And, finally, should be added her prose meditations, composed as well as any of the meditative essays of the seventeenth century.

Anne Bradstreet was ahead of her time. Long before it was accepted as the subject for poetry, nature was both her consolation and her inspiration. In "Contemplations," she was a true Romantic poet generations before Tompson or Bryant, Wordsworth or Emerson.

Warm critical acceptance of the poetry of Anne Bradstreet is growing through the years. She left a notable heritage not only for her children but for all of us. The sententious eulogies by her contemporaries are inappropriate to one so modest in character and purpose, but we are certain that her best poetry, in the effusive words of the Reverend John Norton, will find "its worth in Fame's eternal Almanack."

Notes and References

Citations in the chapter "The Apprentice," because it analyzes the work of the amateur, refer to *The Tenth Muse.* Other citations refer, at their appropriate times, to other editions. It should be noted, however, that the second edition of 1678 and the fourth, or Ellis, edition of 1867 are the same, to all intents and purposes, except for the Ellis additions. Ellis follows his source very closely, making only minor changes, mostly in punctuation—and rightly so since there seemed to be little "science" in Bradstreetian commas and periods. Since errors in this matter serve only to annoy the reader, the Ellis corrections will be followed, unless otherwise noted.

For the reader's guide, the following symbols are adopted:

F = *The Tenth Muse,* or the first edition of 1650.
S = Second edition, revised by the poet (1678).
E = Ellis (fourth) edition, which incorporated the second
    edition and added the religious meditations and other
    poems (1867).

The texts have been followed closely except in spelling where the "u" and "v" and the "i" and "j" were interchanged. Exact transcription would serve no purpose.

Chapter One

1. Cf. Ellis, p. xiv. The supposition is based upon the fact that Northampton was the home of Dudley. Some biographers avoid the issue by the true but brief statement that "she was born in England."

2. Cf. Ellis, pp. xii ff.; Campbell, Chaps. I, II, and many other sources.

3. Winthrop, *Journal,* pp. 23-48.

4. Anne Bradstreet's "His Epitaph" to her father. S., p. 219.

5. See Thomas Goddard Wright, *Literary Culture in Early New England*, p. 44.

6. In 1956, Abbott Lowell Cummings, Assistant Director of the Society for the Preservation of New England Antiquities, proved that the architecture of the house long considered "the Bradstreet house" was not of the period in which they lived. (Boston *Herald*, October 28, 1956.)

Chapter Two

1. From "To My Dear Children," a confessional letter introducing a manuscript left in the hands of Reverend Simon Bradstreet, her son, and printed for the first time in the Ellis edition of 1867. *E.*, p. 3.

2. John Berryman, *Homage to Mistress Bradstreet* (New York, 1956), Stanzas 15, 11, respectively.

3. Louis B. Wright, "The Purposeful Reading of Our Colonial Ancestors," *A Journal of English Literary History*, IV, no. 2 (June, 1937), 92. See also Raleigh's Preface to his *History*, p. 3.

4. Sir Walter Raleigh, *The History of the World*, (At London Printed for Walter Burre, 1614), Bk. III, Chap. I, 17.

5. *Ibid.*, III, 6, 11, 63.

6. S., p. 124.

7. *Ibid.*, p. 88.

8. *Ibid.*, p. 143.

9. *Ibid.*, p. 70.

10. *Ibid.*, p. 1. The reference is evidently to a work by her father, not extant.

11. *Ibid.*, p. 47.

12. *Ibid.*, p. 45.

13. *Ibid.*, p. 3. "The Prologue." Cf. "sugred, sacred Rimes" in John Vicar's *Sacrem Memoriae . . . Josuae Sylvester* among poems introducing the 1641 edition of Sylvester's translation of Du Bartas.

14. *Ibid.*, p. 206. "To Thomas Dudley," p. 2.

15. Cf. Grant C. Knight, *American Literature and Culture* (New York, 1932), p. 43. "A pardonable homesickness for

England shows now and then through the verses she wrote as a solace for her duties."

16. *S.,* p. 233. The vanity of worldly things was, of course, a favorite subject for poets of the Elizabethan and seventeenth-century periods.

17. *S.,* p. 235.

18. *Ibid.,* p. 236.

19. From the confessional letter, *E.,* p. 3.

20. *E.,* pp. 11ff.

21. *Ibid.,* pp. 12ff.

22. *Ibid.,* pp. 6ff.

23. "Meditations Divine and morall," *E.,* pp. 48ff. Meditation I.

24. *Ibid.,* Med. XLVIII. This philosophy of superiority is, of course, a neat application of the belief in the divine right of kings.

25. *Ibid.,* Med. LXV.

26. *Ibid.,* Med. LXVII.

27. *Ibid.,* pp. 20ff.

28. *Ibid.,* p. 42. Compare the first line of this poem with Plangus' lament in Sidney's *Arcadia,* "Alas how long this pilgrimage doth last?" Both he and the other weary pilgrim are aware of life's burdens and man's mortality. The Bradstreet pilgrim, however, looks with hope to another life in which she will be freed of mortal cares. Compare also Robert Herrick's line near the end of *Hesperides*: "A wearied pilgrim, I have wandered here."

Chapter Three

1. *D.A.B.*

2. Percy Boynton, *Literature and American Life* (Boston, 1936), p. 57. Prof. Boynton, however, fairly and enthusiastically praises her later work. See chapter six of this study.

3. Cf. Ellis, p. xli.

4. "The Four Ages of Man," *F.,* p. 43.

5. "The Four Elements," *F.,* p. 5.

6. For their pattern of debate, "The Four Elements" and "The Four Humours" may owe some debt to such medieval literature as "The Owl and the Nightingale," in which the two birds argue their respective superiority. Though they are

birds, they have the characteristics of human beings with their virtues and frailties. "The birds abuse each other about their nature as birds, and all the time the standard is man." Cf. Eric Gerald Stanley, *The Owl and the Nightingale* (New York, 1960), p. 31.

7. Choler, *F.*, pp. 23-26.

8. *F.*, p. 35.

9. *F.*, p. 40. It is interesting that Anne Bradstreet's wish for unity is emphasized in her revised edition where she not only italicizes "Unity" but also capitalizes it.

10. Thomas Hutchinson, *The History of Massachusetts* (Boston, 1795), I, 61-63.

11. *Ibid.*, p. 71.

12. Cf. John Richard Green, *A Short History of the English People* (New York, 1926), II, 508ff.

13. "A Dialogue . . .," *F.*, pp. 180-90. It is quite possible that Anne Bradstreet may have been acquainted with John Bale's *King Johan,* in which the character of "Yngland" pleads the cause of justice before King Johan against clerical and secular corruptions in office, especially the unholy alliance of the two. See John Bale, *King Johan* (The Malone Society Reprints, 1931).

14. "The Four Ages of Man," *F.*, pp. 41-55.

15. "The Four Seasons of the Year," *F.*, pp. 56-64.

16. *F.*, p. 64.

17. "The Four Monarchies" may, indeed, have been a postscript to the preceding quaternions. Her apology for her "bare subject" after "The Four Seasons" indicates reason enough for ending her long poems. But she composes "The Four Monarchies," the longest, the most laboriously written, the most unpromising of all her work, the piece that condemned her in the eyes of future generations, yet the most praised by her contemporaries. She does not get far into the Roman Empire before she quits, exhausted. Was she compelled to write a Christian's history of the world to justify herself as a Puritan poet, especially a Puritan woman poet?

18. *F.*, pp. 178ff.

19. See footnotes 6 and 13.

20. *Op. cit.*, p. xvi.

21. See "The Four Ages of Man."

22. *Du Bartas His Divine Weekes and Workes with A Compleat Collection of all the other most delightfull Workes Translated and written by famous Philomusus Josuah Sylvester gent.* (London printed by Robert Young with Additions, 1641), p. 2.

The original Du Bartas reads:

Le monde est un theatre, où de Dieu la puissance,
La justice, l'amour, le scavoir, la prudence.
Jouent leur personnage . . .

The quotation is from *The Works of Guillaume De Salluste Sieur Du Bartas,* edited by Urban Tigner Holmes *et al.* (Chapel Hill, 1938), II, 199ff. The first edition of 1574 was used. Sylvester's translation was forty-one years after Shakespeare's use of the figure; Du Bartas' original sixteen years before.

23. *F.,* p. 47.

24. Seneca's tragedies were in Increase Mather's library.

25. See Ellis, p. xlv.

26. *F.,* p. 146.

27. *F.,* p. 105.

28. In the second edition, she changed "festivity" to "feastivity."

29. From Tottel's *Songes and Sonettes.* Reprinted in *The Oxford Book of Sixteenth Century Verse* (Oxford, 1932), p. 109. The first stanza reads:

Vain is the fleeting wealth
Whereon the world stays,
Sith stalking time by privy stealth
Encroacheth on our days . . .

30. *Ibid.,* pp. 148-50. From "Respice Finem": "Your world is vain; no trust in earth you find. . . ."

31. *Ibid.,* p. 229.

Chapter Four

1. "The Author to her Book," *S.,* p. 236. *E.,* p. 389.

2. *S.,* p. 32. *F.,* p. 31.

3. *S.*, p. 216. *F.*, p. 205.
4. *S.*, p. 92. *F.*, p. 88.
5. *S.*, p. 30. *F.*, p. 29.
6. *S.*, p. 49. *F.*, p. 46.
7. *S.*, p. 56. *F.*, p. 53.
8. *S.*, p. 57. *F.*, p. 54.
9. *S.*, p. 51. *F.*, p. 48.
10. *S.*, p. vi. *F.*, n. p.
11. *S.*, pp. 9ff.
12. *S.*, p. 57. *F.*, p. 54.
13. Introductory note. *S.*, p. 237. *E.*, p. 391.
14. It has been assumed by some critics that in writing these religious poems she was indebted to Wither. She was undoubtedly familiar with his sacred songs, but a more direct source is surely to be found in the Bay Psalm Book, especially since there are parallel passages between her psalms and those of the Puritan edition.
15. *E.*, p. 12.
16. *E.*, p. 11.
17. *E.*, p. 27.
18. *E.*, pp. 40-42.
19. *S.*, pp. 245-49. *E.*, pp. 400-3.
20. "Upon my dear and loving husband his goeing into England. Jan. 16, 1661." *E.*, p. 33.
21. *S.*, p. 240. *E.*, p. 394.
22. *S.*, pp. 243ff. *E.*, pp. 397ff.
23. *S.*, pp. 239ff. *E.*, pp. 393ff.
24. *S.*, pp. 241ff. *E.*, pp. 395ff.
25. *S.*, pp. 229-33. *E.*, pp. 381-85.
26. "The Debate of the Body and the Soul," in Jessie L. Weston, *The Chief Middle English Poets* (New York, 1914), pp. 304-10.
27. *S.*, p. 220. *E.*, p. 369.
28. *S.*, pp. 217-19. *E.*, pp. 365-68.
29. *S.*, p. 250. *E.*, p. 406.
30. *S.*, pp. 249ff. *E.*, p. 405.
31. See note, *E.*, p. lxvii.
32. *S.*, pp. 250ff. *E.*, pp. 407ff.
33. *S.*, p. 248. *E.*, 404.

34. S., pp. 221-29. *E.*, pp. 371-81.

35. Rev. ii. 17. " 'He who has an ear, let him hear what the Spirit says to the churches. To him who conquers I will give some of the hidden manna, and I will give him a white stone, with a new name written on the stone which no one knows except him who receives it.' "

36. "Contemplations," Stanza 33, S., p. 229. *E.*, p. 381.

37. *Ibid.*, 17, S., p. 225. *E.*, p. 375.

38. *Ibid.*, 4, S., p. 223. *E.*, p. 371.

39. *Ibid.*, 17, S., p. 225. *E.*, p. 375.

40. *Ibid.*, 18, S., p. 225. *E.*, p. 376.

41. *Ibid.*, 22, S., p. 226. *E.*, p. 377.

Chapter Five

Mr. Buchanan Charles was the first to point out that Ellis' transcription of the meditations from the manuscript, while admirably done, was in a few instances in error. Mr. Charles made about fifty corrections, nearly half of which involve punctuation. The errors in the Ellis transcription are due to blotted or blurred lines. None of Mr. Charles' corrections apply to the meditations quoted in this book except for a question about the punctuation after "Commonwealth" in Meditation LXII.

1. The more likely pattern is Quarles' *Enchirideon*, which is composed of similar short, didactic paragraphs.

2. *E.*, p. 47.

3. *Ibid.*

4. *Ibid.*, p. 73.

Chapter Six

1. Winthrop's *Journal*, ed. James Kendall Hosmer (*Original Narratives of Early America*, New York, 1959), II, 225.

2. *F.*, Introductory poem, n. p., S., p. v. *E.*, pp. 85ff.

3. S., pp. vi ff. *E.*, p. 86ff.

4. *F.*, Introductory note, *E.*, p. 90.

5. *F.*, p. 4. S., p. 4.

6. Du Bartas, *op. cit.*, "Indignis" n. p.

7. Elizabeth Wade White, "The Tenth Muse—A Ter-

centenary Appraisal of Anne Bradstreet," *The William and Mary Quarterly,* VIII (July, 1951), 366ff.

8. F. L. Pattee, *Century Readings in American Literature* (New York, 1932), Introduction. Mr. Pattee, although feeling she is not for modern times, does perceive Anne Bradstreet's potential distinction and her pioneering recognition of nature as the subject of poetry. "In other times, indeed, she might have become a lyrist of real distinction. . . . The American landscape awakened in her something new and original. She became one of the first in all English literature to put actual wild nature into her poetry, nature described with enthusiasm and with the eye of the poet actually upon the landscape. *The Four Seasons* and her *Contemplations* were written a full generation before the poems of the Countess of Winchelsea hailed by Wordsworth as the pioneer in the field of English nature poetry of the modern type, and almost a century before the work of Thomson."

9. White, pp. 375ff. Miss White not only points out that Anne Bradstreet's poetry was published before that of Katharine Philips, but that Anne's removal to America spared her "the traditional confinements and artificial multiplicity of the kind of life she would have led in the mother country . . . and the super-imposed classical formalism" that makes Katharine Philips' poetry "all but unreadable to-day."

10. Benét and Pearson, eds., *The Oxford Anthology of American Literature* (New York, 1938), p. 1582.

11. Moses Coit Tyler, *History of American Literature* ("During the Colonial Time"), pp. 179ff.

12. *Ibid.,* p. 292.

13. George Frisbie Whicher, "Alas, All's Vanity or A Leaf from the first American edition of Several Poems by Anne Bradstreet," printed at Boston, anno 1678, p. 7.

14. *Ibid.,* pp. 16ff.

15. Boynton, p. 57.

Selected Bibliography

BIBLIOGRAPHIES

JANTZ, HAROLD S. *The First Century of New England Verse.* New York: Russell and Russell, 1962, p. 183.

SPILLER, ROBERT E., *et al. Literary History of the United States.* New York: Macmillan, 1948, IV.

SVENSON, J. KESTER. "Anne Bradstreet in England: A Bibliographical Note." *American Literature,* XIII (March, 1941), 63-65.

WEGELIN, OSCAR. "A List of Editions of the Poems of Anne Bradstreet, with Some Additional Books Relating to Her." *Am. Book Col.,* IV (July, 1933), 15-16.

PRIMARY SOURCES

The only extant manuscript in Anne Bradstreet's handwriting is in the Stevens Memorial Library at North Andover, Massachusetts. It is the one written for her son Simon, and it contains "Meditations Divine and morall," introduced by the letter to Simon. Also contained in this manuscript is an addition, in Simon's handwriting, of her poems and letters of religious experiences. This is the manuscript used and carefully described by John Harvard Ellis in his edition of the prose and poems. A copy of the manuscript is in the Houghton Library at Harvard. It was one evidently owned by Sarah Bradstreet, whose signature is on the fly-leaf.

BRADSTREET, (MRS.) ANNE. *The Tenth Muse Lately sprung up in America. Or Severall Poems, compiled with great variety of Wit and Learning, full of delight. Wherein especially is contained a compleat discourse and description of The Four Elements, Constitutions, Ages of Man, Seasons of the Year. Together with an Exact Epitomie of the four Monarchies, viz. The Assyrian, Persian,*

Grecian, Roman. Also a Dialogue between Old England and New, concerning the late troubles. With divers other pleasant and serious Poems. By a Gentlewoman in those parts. Printed at London for Stephen Bowtell at the signe of the Bible in Popes Head-Alley, 1650.

————. *Several Poems Compiled with great variety of Wit and Learning, full of Delight; Wherein especially is contained a compleat Discourse, and Description of The Four Elements, Constitutions, Ages of Man, Seasons of the Year. Together with an exact Epitome of the three first Monarchyes Viz. The Assyrian, Persian, Grecian. And beginning of the Romane Common-wealth to the end of their last King: With diverse other Pleasant & serious Poems,* By a Gentlewoman in New-England. The second Edition, Corrected by the Author, and enlarged by an Addition of several other Poems found amongst her Papers after her Death. Boston, Printed by John Foster, 1678.

————. *Several Poems Compiled with great Variety of Wit and Learning, full of Delight; Wherein especially is contained, a compleat Discourse and Description of The Four Elements, Constitutions, Ages of Man, Seasons of the Year. Together with an exact Epitome of the three first Monarchies, viz. the Assyrian, Persian, Grecian, and Roman Common Wealth, from its beginning to the End of their last King. With divers other pleasant and serious Poems.* By a Gentlewoman in New-England. The Third Edition, corrected by the Author, and enlarged by an Addition of several other Poems found amongst her Papers after her Death. Re-printed from the second Edition in the Year M. DCC. LVIII.

————. *The Works of Anne Bradstreet, in Prose and Verse.* Edited by John Harvard Ellis. Charlestown: A. E. Cutter, 1867.

————. *The Poems of Mrs. Anne Bradstreet* (1612-1672). *Together with Her Prose Remains with An Introduction by Charles Eliot Norton.* The Duodecimos, MDCCCXCVII. Critical of Ellis' exact reprint. Offers edition in which "orthography, especially of proper names, has been care-

fully modernized, in which evident printers' errors have been corrected, and a few trifling alterations made to avoid perpetuating instances of unnecessarily bad grammar,—defects which can add no value to a new edition, but obscure such meaning as the lines may contain . . . elided letters have been supplied in accordance with modern usages. The reader will understand that the meter requires the slurred pronunciation formerly indicated by the apostrophe . . ." The tone of the editor is one of condescension.

————. Reprint of Ellis edition. Peter Smith, Gloucester, Mass., 1932.

————. Reprint. Peter Smith, Gloucester, Mass., 1962. "'A Dialogue . . .' and other poems." Old South Leaflets, No. 159.

SECONDARY SOURCES

Biography and Criticism

There are so many excellent critical discussions of the Bradstreet poetry in literary histories, such as Tyler's, and anthologies of American literature, such as those edited by Conrad Aiken and Benét and Pearson, that it is impossible to list them all here. There has appeared in such sources a real recognition of the place of Anne Bradstreet in American literature.

Anderson, Cole, and Taylor, cited below, are chiefly interested in the poet as a delightful and surprising phenomenon of the Puritan period in New England.

Anderson, Rev. James. *Memorable Women of Puritan Times.* London: 1861.

Berryman, John. *Homage to Mistress Bradstreet.* New York: Farrar, Straus and Cudahy, 1956. This is a remarkable poetic interpretation (based upon the reading of her poetry) of the mind of Anne Bradstreet as she experiences the joys and sorrows of her life in New England. It was written under a Guggenheim grant, and was first published in *The Partisan Review.*

BRADSTREET, METTA. "Anne Bradstreet: Her Life and Works," *Historical Collections, Topsfield, Massachusetts.* Published by the Society, 1895. Written by a descendant of Anne Bradstreet, the work is disappointing in that it is a short review of facts, which are at best few, concerning her life. The appreciation of her work in this short essay is merely perfunctory.

CALDWELL, COL. LUTHER. *An Account of Anne Bradstreet, the Puritan Poetess and Kindred Topics.* Boston, Damrell & Upham, 1898. A sentimental rather than scholarly account. "It is the object of this little volume to make the Puritan mother-poetess, the beloved and loving wife, and the Christian woman better known to the people of Ipswich at home and abroad. It is published as a work of love, and not for profit or gain." He does point to a fact, not too often emphasized, that she "was as talented a prose writer as in versification." This book is of interest as one of the persistent revivals of interest in Anne Bradstreet.

CAMPBELL, HELEN (STUART). *Anne Bradstreet and Her Time.* Boston: D. Lothrop Company, 1891. More about Anne Bradstreet's time than about her life.

COLE, PAMELA McARTHUR. "Notable New England Women," *New England Magazine* (July, 1887), 63-70.

CUTTER, ABRAM E. *Bradstreetiana.* August 10, 1907. A scrapbook from the estate of Cutter, the publisher of the Ellis edition of 1867. The collection of clippings and letters is in the Boston Public Library.

FUESS, CLAUDE M. "Andover's Anne Bradstreet, Puritan Poet," *Andover Symbol of New England.* Andover Historical Society and North Andover Historical Society, 1959. Anne Bradstreet is shown as one of the symbols of Andover and of New England culture.

JANTZ, HAROLD S. *The First Century of New England Verse.* New York: Russell and Russell, 1962, 36-38. Recognizes her charm and her real ability as a poet.

MAKIN, BATHSUA. *An Essay to Revive the Ancient Education of Gentlewomen in Religion, Manners, Arts & Tongues.* London, J. D. to be sold by Tho. Parkhurst, 1673. Within this essay is Mrs. Makin's appreciation of Anne Bradstreet. The book is of interest as evidence of her recognition abroad.

MATHER, COTTON. *Magnalia Christi Americana*. London, Printed for Thomas Parkhurst, 1702; Hartford, Roberts & Burry Printers, 1820. Pages 133-34 of the American edition deal with Dudley's life in England. It is followed by effusive praise of Dudley's daughter (pp. 134-35) "whose poems, divers times printed, have afforded a grateful entertainment into the ingenious, and a monument for her memory beyond the statliest marbles."

MORISON, SAMUEL ELIOT. "Mistress Anne Bradstreet," *Builders of the Bay Colony*. Boston: Houghton Mifflin Riverside Press, 1930. An expert appraisal of Anne Bradstreet's poetry in American letters.

————. "Verse," *The Puritan Pronaos*. New York: New York University Press, 1936. Published in 1956 by the Cornell University Press, as one of its Great Seal Books, under the title, *The Intellectual Life of Colonial New England*.

NORTON, JOHN. "A Funeral Elogy, Upon that Pattern and Patron of Virtue, the truly pious, peerless and matchless Gentlewoman Mrs. Anne Bradstreet." September, 1672. Printed in the second edition of her poems.

PHILLIPS, EDWARD (nephew of John Milton). "Women among the Moderns Eminent for Poetry," *Theatrum Poetarum*. London: Printed for Charles Smith, 1675. Like Mrs. Makin's, this book is of particular interest for its recognition in England of Anne Bradstreet's poetry.

RICHARDSON, LYON N. "Anne Bradstreet," *Dictionary of American Biography*. The known facts of her life. Not very appreciative of her poetry.

TAYLOR, JOHN PHELPS. *A Historical Discourse*. Preached in the Seminary Chapel, Andover, May 7, 1896. Being the Sunday Prior to the 250th Anniversary of the Incorporation of the Town. The Andover Press. Eulogies of three noted people in Andover's history: Anne Bradstreet, Samuel Phillips, Eliphalet Pearson.

TYLER, MOSES COIT. *A History of American Literature During the Colonial Period*. New York: G. P. Putnam's Sons, 1897, I, 277-92. Tyler remains one of the best historians and critics of American literature for his knowledge of historical background and his perceptive criticism. He is one of the earliest critics to give full recognition to Anne Bradstreet.

VANCURA, Z. "Baroque Prose in America," *Studies in English.* Charles University (Prague), IV (1935), 39-88. A discussion of seventeenth-century baroque prose, in which the stylistic manner of writing is quite as important as the content. It is characterized by the use of sentences that are balanced and concise, images that are sharp, and metaphors that are vivid, often elaborated into a conceit. The style, carried to extremes, is illustrated in the seventeenth-century metaphysical writers. In Anne Bradstreet's prose meditations, he sees the characteristic stylistic efforts in the aphorism, the balanced sentence, the neatly turned phrase, the apt metaphor.

WHICHER, GEORGE F., ed. *Alas, All's Vanity, or, A Leaf from the First American Edition of Several Poems by Anne Bradstreet* printed at Boston, anno 1678. With an essay by George Frisbie Whicher now printed in 1942 at the Spiral Press for publication by Collectors' Bookshop. New York. An excellent appreciation of the Bradstreet poetry, quoted in the last chapter of this book.

WHITE, ELIZABETH WADE. "A Study of the Life and Works of Anne Bradstreet, 1612-1672." B. Litt. thesis, St. Hilda's, Oxford, 1952-53.

————. "The Tenth Muse—A Tercentenary Appraisal of Anne Bradstreet," *The William and Mary Quarterly,* VIII, No. 3 (July, 1951). A particular emphasis on the appreciation of Anne Bradstreet by English contemporaries and the establishment of Anne Bradstreet as the first significant woman poet of the English language.

WHITE, TRENTWELL MASON, and P. W. LEHMAN. *Writers of Colonial New England.* Boston: Palmer Company, 1929. The not too infrequent conclusion that Anne Bradstreet lived under the rigid rules of Puritanism so completely that "Jonson and Shakespeare, Fletcher and Shirley, meant only examples of the Devil's ingenuity." The authors find in her early poetry "the usual puns and fantastic figures learned from Quarles, Du Bartas and Wither." They find in "The Dialogue of Old England and New" the "apostle of freedom, an avenging angel, a vitriol-tongued champion of the oppressed, a fighter for women's rights as well as men's. . . . Bitter sarcasm, biting wit, and crackling epigram play across the pages of this poem." On the whole, this is a vigorous piece of criticism of the Bradstreet poetry.

WILLIAMS, STANLEY T. "The Beginnings of American Poetry (1620-1855)." The Gottesman Lectures, Uppsala University (Uppsala and Stockholm, n. d.). Lecture in 1948; preface dated 1951. Criticism slanted toward foreign students totally unfamiliar with the beginnings of our literature.

Background

There are, of course, many chapters and books on the history of the times that can give the student a feeling for the background to the study of Anne Bradstreet. This is a very brief list.

CUMMINGS, ABBOTT LOWELL. "Not Anne Bradstreet House," *Boston Herald,* October 28, 1956. Mr. Cummings, Assistant Director of the Society for the Preservation of New England Antiquities, proved that the architecture of the house long considered "the Bradstreet house" was not of the period in which Anne Bradstreet lived.

FIEDELSON, CHARLES, JR. *Symbolism and American Literature.* University of Chicago Press, Phoenix Books, 1953. Chap. III, "An American Tradition," is good for an analysis of Puritan thought in America.

FLAVEL, JOHN. *Husbandry Spiritualized; or the Heavenly Use of Earthly Things.* Witham: Printed for and Sold by P. Youngman, 1805. The first edition published in 1669 may have influenced Anne Bradstreet to use in her "Meditations" figures of speech derived from familiar things.

MATHER, COTTON. *Magnalia Christi Americana* (London). In spite of Mather's verbosity and his self-importance, one can always derive a good deal of knowledge about his period and his contemporaries from his Magnalia. The biographies of Bradstreet and Dudley are cases in point.

MILLER, PERRY. "Poetry," The American Puritans, Their Prose and Poetry. New York: Doubleday Anchor, 1956. Mr. Miller has long been an authority on American prose and poetry of the New England colonial period.

MORGAN, EDMUND S. The Puritan Dilemma: The Story of John Winthrop. Boston: Little, Brown and Company, 1958. A study of how the circumstances of difficult living in New England and the consequent necessity of a closely knit society circumscribed the ideas of religious freedom with which the Puritans came to America. "The result was a long conflict between the demands of authority and the permissiveness of freedom" (Oscar Handlin, Editor's Preface).

MURDOCK, KENNETH B. Literature and Theology in Colonial New England. Cambridge: Harvard University Press, 1949. To the Puritan, "theology was . . . the noblest of sciences." And since he had come to America to establish a new Canaan and to propagate the gospel on a new continent, he found his means of expressing his mission in theological writing that had already found its Golden Age abroad.

NOTESTEIN, WALLACE. The English People on the Eve of Colonization, 1603-1630. New York: Harper and Bros., 1954. A good study of the motivations of colonization.

SCHNEIDER, HERBERT W. The Puritan Mind. Ann Arbor: University of Michigan Press, 1958. A philosophical analysis of the Puritan mind and the influences upon it.

STEWART, RANDALL. American Literature and Christian Doctrine. Baton Rouge: Louisiana State University Press, 1958. Like Murdock and Schneider, Mr. Stewart is interested in the philosophical implications of early New England writing. However, all three authors give their subject a fresh approach, and all are "musts" in understanding this period. Mr. Stewart's thesis is that not free thinking but deep religious belief is the basis of our literature and our national culture.

Selected Bibliography

TYLER, MOSES COIT. *A History of American Literature During the Colonial Period.* New York: G. P. Putnam's Sons, 1879.

WILLEY, BASIL. *The Seventeenth Century Background.* New York: Doubleday Anchor Book, 1955. Though concerned with influences on philosophical thought abroad, it is always an excellent study for ideas of the seventeenth century at home or abroad.

WINTHROP, JOHN. *Winthrop's Journal,* in *History of New England, 1630-1649.* Edited by James Kendall Hosmer. New York: Barnes & Noble, Inc., 1959. History in the making, a record of the first governor of the Massachusetts Bay Colony from the time that he and others, including Anne Bradstreet, put out from England.

WRIGHT, LOUIS B. *The Colonial Civilization of North America, 1607-1763.* London: Eyre and Spottiswoode, 1949. Published in America under the title *The Atlantic Frontier.* Ithaca: Cornell University Press, 1947. With the added introductory chapter "The Old World Background."

————. "The Purposeful Reading of our Colonial Ancestors," *A Journal of English Literary History,* IV, No. 2 (June, 1937), 85-111. The purpose of reading among our New England ancestors, especially in history, was to derive moral lessons.

WRIGHT, THOMAS GODDARD. *Literary Culture in Early New England, 1620-1730.* New Haven: Yale University Press, 1920. An invaluable book not only for a scholarly presentation of our early culture, but for statistical evidence through documents showing the colonists' interest in personal libraries.

Index

Index

66ff.; "To the Memory of my dear and ever honoured Father Thomas Dudley, Esq." 78, 91; "An Epitaph On my dear and ever honoured Mother," 78, 91; "In Memory of my dear grandchild Anne Bradstreet," 92; "In memory of my dear grandchild Elizabeth," 94ff.; "To the memory of my dear Daughter in Law, Mrs. Mercy Bradstreet," 92ff.; "On my dear Grandchild Simon Bradstreet"

Elizabeth, Queen, 17, 22, 23, 111; "In Honour of that High and Mighty Princess Queen Elizabeth of Happy Memory," 66ff.

Elizabethan background, 22; playwrights, 59

Ellis, John Harvard, 8, 30, 34, 59, 70, 114, 117

Emblematic literature, 102-3

Emerson, Ralph Waldo, 101, 120

Endicott, John, 46ff.

"An Epitaph On my dear and ever honoured Mother," 78, 91

"The Flesh and the Spirit," 78, 88-90

Fletcher, Phineas, 94, 100

"For the restoration of my dear Husband from a burning Ague, June, 1661," 81

"Four Ages of Man," 31, 41, 54ff., 73

"The Four Elements," 42ff., 49

"The Four Humours," 43-55, 66, 72

"Four Monarchies," 23, 24, 32, 56, 63, 72, 115

"The Four Seasons," 41, 55-56, 64

Galileo, 21

Hippocratic scheme of elements, humours, ages of man, 42

Humours, 43-55, 66, 72

Hutchinson, Anne, 28, 29, 47, 48, 49

"I had eight birds hatcht in one nest," 82ff.

"In memory of my dear grandchild Anne Bradstreet," 92

"In memory of my dear grandchild Elizabeth Bradstreet," 94ff.

"In thankfull Remembrance for my dear husbands safe Arrival, Sept. 3, 1662," 83

Jonson, Ben, 22

Kepler, 22

Lanier, Sidney, 119

Laud, Archbishop, 19, 51

"A Letter to her Husband, absent upon Publick employment" (Ellis' title), 84ff.

Libraries, Bradstreet, 23, 24; Dudley, 23; Lincoln, 23

Lincoln, Earl of, 17, 18, 19, 23, 77

London fire, 76ff.

Love poems, 84-90

Lyrical Ballads, The, 82

Makin, Mrs. Bathsua (*An Essay to Revive the Ancient Education of Gentlewomen in Religion, Manners, Arts & Tongues*), 113

Marlowe, Christopher, 22

Mather, Cotton (*Christian Philosopher*), 101, 103; Richard, 79

Medieval debate literature, 9; "The Debate of the Body and Soul," 90; "The Owl and the Nightingale," 90, 123 n. 6, Chapter Three

Meditations ("Meditations Divine and morall"), 78, 103; Occasional meditations, 78

Merrimac, 7

Index

Millay, Edna St. Vincent, 119
Milton, John ("On the Death of a
  Fair Infant Dying of a Cough"),
  95
Monarchies, The Four, 23, 26, 30,
  56
Morison, S. E., 88, 90, 118ff.
"My Subjects bare, my Brains are
  bad," 56
"My thankful heart with glorying
  Tongue," 81

Newtown (Cambridge), 7, 18
Norton, Charles Eliot, 114; Rev.
  John Norton, 120

"Occasional Meditations," see
  "Meditations"
"Of the Vanity of all worldly
  creatures," 33, 34, 69-72
"On the Vanity of Man's Life"
  (anonymous Elizabethan poem),
  70
[On the burning of her house], 82
"The Owl and the Nightingale"
  (medieval debate literature),
  90, 123 n. 6, Chapter Three

Pattee, F. L., 114, 128 n. 8
Pearson, Norman Holmes, 116
Philips, Katharine, 116
Phillips, Edward, 112
Play upon words, 61-63
Plutarch, 58
Poems in praise of Anne Brad-
  street; contemporary, 111-13;
  modern, 113-15
Politics, Anne Bradstreet's inter-
  est in, see "Dialogue between
  Old England and New," 51-54
Proctor, Thomas ("Respice Fin-
  em"), 70; ("A Proper Sonnet,
  Low Time Consumeth All
  Things"), 70
Psalms, see The Bay Psalm Book
Puritan, Puritans, 22, 48, 60, 110,
  115, 116, 119; Adam, 31, 32, 33,

97; doctrine, 20-22, 29, 36-38;
  Doctrines accepted by Anne, 36-
  38; government, 50ff.

Quarles, Francis, 102; Enchirideon,
  127 n. 1, Chapter V
Quaternions, see the "four times
  four poems": "The Four Ages
  of Man," "The Four Elements,"
  "The Four Humours," "The
  Four Seasons"

Raleigh, Sir Walter, 22, 26, 63,
  115; History of the World, 23,
  29, 30, 31, 32, 58, 63, 65
Revisions for second edition, 74-77
Romantic poets (Anne Bradstreet's
  lyric poetry, resemblance to
  romantic poetry), 81

Salem, 18
Savelle, Max. (Seeds of Liberty,
  criticism of Bradstreet poetry),
  114
Seasons, see "The Four Seasons"
Sempringham, residence of Earl of
  Lincoln, 18
Seneca, 63
Shakespeare, influences, 9, 22, 64;
  As You Like It, 59, 60; Antony
  and Cleopatra, 61, 87; King
  Lear, 61; Winter's Tale, 61;
  Sonnets 95, 98
Shelley, Percy Bysshe, 101
Sidney, Sir Philip, 100, 111; "An
  Elegie upon that Honourable
  and renowned Knight Sir
  Philip Sidney, who was untime-
  ly slain at the Siege of Zutphen,
  Anno, 1586," 66, 67; Arcadia,
  123 n. 28; Astrophel and Stella,
  87ff.
Spenser, "An Hymne in Honour of
  Beauty," 89
Sylvester, Joshua; translator of Du
  Bartas, 29, 59